I Always Dreamed of Flying

A Songwriter's Autobiography

By

Bob Grubel

Copyright © 2023 by Bob Grubel

All rights reserved.

No part of this publication may be reproduced, distributed, or transmitted in any form or by any means, including photocopying, recording, or other electronic or mechanical methods, without the prior written permission of the publisher, except as permitted by U.S. copyright law. For permission requests, contact Bob Grubel (singnbob@hotmail.com).

For privacy reasons, some names, locations, and dates may have been changed.

ISBN: 979-8-9894324-0-0 (Paperback)
ISBN: 979-8-9894324-1-7 (Ebook)

Cover Art and Design by Amy Avery-Grubel

Back Cover Photo by Jerry Schrader

Proofreaders: Jim Scott, Rick Wilsterman, Sandy Burg, Amy Avery-Grubel

Formatted by Amy Avery-Grubel

Published by Zephyr Publications

First Edition, 2023

Almost all the songs mentioned in this book are available for listening and download on www.BobGrubel.com. They also can be found on most popular streaming services by entering Bob Grubel and the song title. If you wish to hear any Grace Note material, you must enter "Grace Note Bob Grubel" and the song title.

Please feel free to contact me at singnbob@hotmail.com. I welcome any communication!

CONTENTS

Foreword i
Acknowledgements v
Introduction vii
SOWING THE SEEDS 1
    Discovery 9
    Community Evolution 11
    California Beckons 18
    Lessons Learned 22
    Calling Calling 28
    Arrival at Zephyr 39
GARDEN IN BLOOM 50
    Grace Note is Born 60
    Keep the Light Burning 67
    What's Dear 76
    Rivers from the Sun 88
    Dancing in Relationship 92
    Making Peace 120
A RIPENING HARVEST 126
    Interlude 137
    Staying Above the Radar 138
    Pressing Rewind 156
CASTING SEEDS TO THE WIND 159
EPILOGUE 163
Bonus Material 165
    The Recordings 165
    Creative Friends 169
    Vital Characters 170
    Musicians 171

"Weakness is treating someone as though they belong to you. Strength is knowing that everyone belongs to themselves."

Yaa Gyasi, *Homegoing*

Each of us belongs in our own dreams.

Foreword

I met Bob for the first time in the fall of 1968 in the entrance of the college library. We were first year students at Earlham College, a small Quaker school located on the east side of Indiana, near the Ohio line. On one side, a small Midwestern city, and on the other, miles and miles of woods and farmland. You had the feeling of being on an oasis. And, in fact, you were.

While I met many people who would become lifelong friends during this time, Bob is the only one whom I recall meeting. Not only that, but I recall the things we discussed. Why this is so, I can't tell you. But I can tell you this: that meeting Bob left an indelible impression.

It was night and we stood in a corner of light. Bob was long and lanky, and relaxed in the way he held himself. He appeared to be letting his hair grow long for the first time, a sign of the times we lived. He had wide eyes, that seemed to want to take the world in, and a welcoming smile that was ready to laugh.

For a good hour, we talked about young people we met, or knew of, who were living in places such as Greenwich Village, and trying on new lifestyles. There were the Diggers, at Washington Square, who gave away everything they owned. Others, who were organizing small urban collectives and communes. People, seeking new forms of human relations, and ways of relating to each other. All of them seeking antidotes, whether on a personal or societal level, to the culture in which we lived.

It occurs to me, in writing these words, that the stickiness of this particular memory, more than half a century ago, may owe to the sincerity and authenticity I felt in Bob's quest. You knew immediately that he was a searcher, a pilgrim, and as this memoir will show you, a pioneer. And then there was the joy and delight, his, and that which he inspired in me.

I haven't seen Bob since the early 1970's. On one of the last occasions I recall, I stayed for a week in a house Bob and some college friends were renting, in a working-class suburb of Boston. They had dropped out of college together, after second year, and were trying to organize a rock band. They had inspiration and musicianship, and hoped that an abundance of the first would tide them over until they had enough of the second. They played music at night in the basement.

On the second floor of this rambling old house there were four or five elderly women who were left behind when the house, a former nursing home, was sold. They were on their own. Bob and his friends looked after them by feeding them, keeping them company, and running errands. Eventually, Bob and the other band members placed all of them in suitable nursing homes.

This episode is richly recounted in Bob's memoir. Bob was testing his wings for one of the first times, and learning who he was. What we see is compassion, a love of fellowship, and a desire to build community. And we are also introduced to these themes: Bob looks and leaps at the same instant, and not one before the other, and thrives in situations of limited security that allow him to cut his own path forward.

Time passes. And then, about fifteen years ago, Bob and I found each other on social media. We hadn't seen each other for decades, and then, there was Zoom. I suspect that Bob saw about what I saw on our first meeting: we were familiar aliens, one living on Uranus and the other, on Neptune.

Bob was in his home in Zephyr, an intentional community nestled in the forests and hills of Virginia, near the Appalachian Trail. He built the house by hand and surrounded it with gardens that he and Sandy, the love of his life, tend. One of his daughters lives down a road, with family, around a bend and beyond some trees. His family stays close. And he talks about friends, in Zephyr and further beyond, the way most people today talk about family.

If I was on Neptune, it has another name, Rotterdam, Europe's largest port. I am quite sure we both marveled, at the distance during this first meeting, in years, and smiled in our hearts, knowing we would spread a rope around the Atlantic, and pull it in, until we were closer. There are moments when I can feel I am one of Bob's neighbors, in Zephyr.

There is a temptation to see Bob's life, today, by extrapolating from currents that were in the air in the Sixties. Yet, when you read this memoir, you quickly realize that would be missing the point. Bob has always been too creative, too original, and too much an artist to fit into any easy mold or schema. As the nineteenth century English poet, Wordsworth, wrote, "We murder to dissect".

So, I would counsel you, readers, to open yourself to the unexpected when you go through these pages. Nothing ever unfolds quite as you think it will. Let go, as Bob always does, and find your own comfort level with "insecurity", a word Bob nurtures in his life, like something in his garden.

This is not to say that Bob's life story is made of thin air. But only that if you're looking at the Sixties, you're looking in the wrong place. For a more meaningful understanding, you might begin by looking at the trades Bob has mastered. In the memoir, he refers to them as "tools". He leverages them to afford the independence his life requires, and also as an expression of identity and a quest to thread together all parts of his life, to give it ever richer spiritual meaning.

He has been a candlemaker and a potter, a goat farmer and a gardener, a masseur, and of course, a musician. But this only begins the list. Bob is an incessant entrepreneur. In reading these pages I was reminded of a memoir I read many years ago written by an American whose life had spanned much of the nineteenth century. This earlier memoir, on the one hand, was an inventory of trades people did at the time. And, on the other hand, it was a display of something quintessentially American: Something we used to call a "can do" spirit, containing doses of self-reliance, independence, ingenuity, and, amidst it all, joy.

Now, I write these next few words, which will conclude this foreword, as an American who has lived in Europe for many years, and who, at the same time, has a love for history. I have an inside-outside perspective, and, by the nature of things, stand at some distance to what I see.

Bob's life, as reflected in this memoir, expresses more than anything else, and captures better than anyone else I know, an American spirit, a new American man, as expressed by our first original school of philosophy, the Transcendentalists, whose most known adherents were Ralph Waldo Emerson and Henry David Thoreau. They were most active in the 1820s and 1830s. And then, following upon them, the author who invented an American genre of poetry, Walt Whitman, whose "Leaves of Grass" was published in 1855.

Here is Thoreau, writing in "Civil Disobedience": "I went to the woods because I wished to live deliberately, to front only the essential facts of life…and not, when I came to die, discover that I had not lived. I did not wish to live what was not life, living is so dear; nor did I wish to practice resignation".

In another of his works, "Walden", Thoreau gives us these celebrated words, "If a man does not keep pace with his companions, perhaps it is because he hears a different drummer. Let him step to the music which he hears, however measured or far away."

Of course, I cannot resist the reference to music, which Thoreau uses metaphorically. Should you continue in these pages, you will find an original memoir, one which is told twice. Once in prose, and afterwards in song. We don't have the melodies on the written page, of course, but Bob shows us how to find them. But even without the melodies, the songs sing on the written page so that what we find is a memoir written in prose and poetry.

I mentioned Whitman. Does Bob sing "the body electric?" Oh everywhere, just about everywhere.

Joe Goldiamond
July 10, 2023

Acknowledgements

This book would never have come to press without the support of a host of folks. First off! To the people who remain anonymous, who when asking me what I was up to these days and heard about this project consistently cheered me on – here is a huge, big hug and thank you.

As I proceeded along Rick Wilsterman gave me much valuable input and great assistance with editing. That was a steep learning curve! Thank you so much Rick! Several friends and family members popped in suggestions that added character to my writing and some form to the book. Among them was Joe Goldiamond, my sister Betsey Crimmins, my daughter Amy was invaluable, and Jim Scott (whom I asked to do a review and then chipped in worthy critique!) Every little bit was appreciated!

My friend and Focusing partner, Jay-L Fogo, deserves an award for listening to my meanderings with compassion! There were a few moments when life was throwing me curve balls and your presence got me around the bases safely!

My partner in life and love, Sandy Jahmi Burg, was involved from the get go. She offered advice on several aspects of this project and was kind enough to listen to portions as I wrote. She gave me feedback that likely provided a kind of balance I was in need of.

Say hello to the spark that lives within
Growing slow like the flowers in the spring
And you know when it all falls into place
You can't erase taking chances.

From *Fragrance of the Rose*

Introduction

Writing this autobiography was a bit like digging in the dirt is for me. There is a richness of textures, colors, smells and unknown waiting to be unearthed with each shovel turned over. My last name Grubel translates to "little digger" in German. I sit here turning over the dirt of my life, some of it is rich garden soil and some a rocky root filled canal. All of it an exploration of my participation in this gift I have been given, the breath of life.

I was fortunate to have journals to refer to that I have kept from the age of 18 and have somehow followed me to my current residence. There have been moments of intense feelings brought on by memories or reflections on what occurred. I had many deep long conversations with friends and family members whom I consulted about their experiences with me in years past. One day I was on the phone for 8 hours with just 4 people. I owe all of you a deep gratitude.

I started to refer to this process as a life review, as it certainly has become that for me. Many times in my life a song would start up in my dreams and I would rise to capture that gift before it faded away. Writing this has brought about some of the same kind of momentum. I had no idea I could do this when I started. The writing has urged itself upon me.

This book explores my life within the framework of hundreds of songs I wrote in this lifetime loosely guiding the way. If you are still with me here, dear reader, I wish for you some value or affirmation from allowing my experience into your life.

SOWING THE SEEDS

How many mornings have you awakened and been inspired by the dreams you encountered the night before? This morning I realized I needed to write about my life and the songs that have come to me over the past 50 plus years through dreams, conversations, and life in the day-to-day. Not wanting to pass the moment of inspiration, I sat myself down to catch its potency before it faded away. Let me commence with my family roots over 70 years ago.

My parents were married in 1948. After meeting on the steps of the Martha Van Rensselaer building at Cornell in the summer of 1946, they continued to build a relationship while employed in the same high school in Sauquoit, New York. They both grew up on farms and sought other means of employment that involved getting a college education. My dad, Leonard Grubel, was 10 years older than my mom, Margaret Johnson. That was a bit unusual for the era. They wanted to have a large family, but my mom had difficulty carrying babies to term. Eventually, in 1950, I came through, though I was induced due to toxemia. I discovered this about my birth when I was "rebirthed" by Jack Painter (my massage teacher many years later) on my 26th birthday and basically left feeling like I was not ready to come out at the moment of my birth. After the rebirth experience I called my mom and asked her about my birth. That is when I learned I had been induced.

I have two sisters, Betsey and Cindy, the latter of whom was born 12 years after me. She weighed only 3lbs 2oz at birth and she spent the first two months of her life in an incubator. I still remember the anxiety of seeing my mom leave the house in an ambulance to go to the hospital for delivery. I suspect my dad was a lot more anxious.

My sister Betsey, me, and baby Cindy

Dad carves the turkey for Thanksgiving, 1962. Upper row: Dad, me, Uncle Bill, Aunt Nancy, Mom. Betsey in front.

In the early 1950s my parents had a house built on an acre of land on Paris Hill Road in Sauquoit near Utica, New York. I lived in that house for most of my first 18 years. The house was on a street that was filling up with new families and eventually would house a lot of kids my age. We had the run of the neighborhood and engaged in seasonal sports, lots of play and other shared activities. The school we attended was not that large, with about 90 kids in my class. I attended classes with many of the same kids for my entire 12 years of elementary and high school. Several are lifelong friends and played key roles in my life at various times.

I was born into a family that had music as part of its fabric. There was often singing at family gatherings around the Holidays. My sisters and I were required to take piano lessons from the age of 7 or so. I remember vague interest and some trepidation when it came time to perform at recitals. That trepidation moved forward throughout my life when performing live. It would often persist until I would get two to four songs into whatever performance I was bringing into being. Then the music would take over with a life of its own and I would be fine! Over the years I have realized the selection of song order (choosing familiar material to start) or playing with other musicians makes diving in much easier.

When I was in the 3rd grade, I entered our elementary school choir and began a lifetime of singing. While in the 5th grade our teacher, Mrs. Johnson, gave us an assignment to write about what we wanted to do in our lives. I wrote that I wanted to be a musician. Perhaps I was setting the table for what was to follow. I eventually became able to sight read for singing, but never accomplished a great deal of ability reading music to play piano. It was hard work. By the age of 14, I had had enough. I then quit piano lessons in favor of sporting activities.

During all those years, I sang in the school choirs from 3rd grade on. Our choirs were very good and won awards in statewide competitions for schools of our size. My junior year I had to drop out of choir because I grew so much my vocal cords wouldn't let me sing! I went from being 5 feet 6 inches to 6 feet 3 inches in about nine months. I was an alto in 9th grade, a tenor in tenth and a bass by the time I returned in my senior year. I later attributed this growth spurt to several things, but one rather esoteric thing stood out. I had prayed every night starting as a freshman in high school to be 6 feet 3 inches tall so I could be better at basketball. Viola, the power of thought demonstrated itself to me early in life and this became an important lesson. I later sang in choirs at Earlham (the college I attended) and joined a Chamber choir of 16 voices there as well. I actually got to perform in Carnegie Hall with that group when we went on an east coast tour. The love of tight harmonies found its place in me through those many years of singing in choirs.

My dad played the trumpet in a small dance band with his two sisters while growing up. He also led a band while stationed in the Army Air Force during WWII. He was a good musician, but I don't remember ever hearing him play. That may have been in part because he saddled himself with a cigarette addiction that not only shortened his breath but his life as well. My father taught agriculture and vocational arts as they called it back then (shop, welding, small engine repair). While I did take shop from him, I didn't really learn any of those skills until later in life from other people. My dad was very involved in the lives of many farmers in the area, visiting them often on weekends. He also was involved in the Rotary, a Deacon in the church and other civic organizations.

My parents both attempted to feed us all as well as could be understood at the time. When I was young, we had a fairly large garden that shrank as the years went on. My mother continued a small garden almost until the time she had to leave our home in Sauquoit in 2013. I believe this instilled in me an enthusiasm for gardening that has become a lifelong pursuit.

My mother's side of the family continued to farm until I was 12 years old. The farm was located in a beautiful valley in southern New Hampshire near a small town named Winchester. I spent many hours roaming in the barn,

My favorite cow, she actually let me ride her!

playing in the hayloft and helping feed the cattle or drive them in for milking. I was just getting introduced to farm machinery when my grandfather sold the farm to his brother's son.

My grandfather, S. Guy Johnson, retained 100 acres of forest that he managed as a tree farm. In the spring and the fall for many of the years in my early 20s I would go work with him on the tree farm. I got very adept with a chainsaw. He and I would lie down on the forest floor for a brief nap after our lunch (this was before Lymes disease). That was a precious time for me and in part created a lifetime habit of napping that I still engage in to this day. My grandfather also sang in barbershop quartets and played the viola, but I never witnessed that. I did see him sing in the church choir until he was 86 years old as many other family members did. I remember my grandmother Elsie Johnson most for her cooking, particularly the donuts that were always waiting to greet us when we arrived. I would make a beeline to the pantry where they were stashed. She had a warm countenance, but I honestly don't know much about her life. I do remember this though. For several years after her death in 1965, whenever I was faced with a difficult decision, I would find myself thinking of her and asking for guidance. This eventually abated but introduced me to the thought or feeling that there is more going on here than meets the eye. My grandfather told me that she came to him after her death and told him to be open to

Elsie and Guy Johnson

another relationship because he was going to live for a long time. Within two years he was remarried to a woman who lived in Winchester and moved in with her there. She also had a cabin on a nearby lake that he got to enjoy in the summer months of his retirement. We referred to her as Aunt Ella. He shared the last ten years of his life with her until his death in the fall of 1977.

My grandfather had a new home built for his time of retirement. It was on land that had been part of the farm. When he moved to town with his new wife, my Aunt Mimi moved into the house and lived there until the year 2021. Mimi was always most welcoming to me and I probably shared almost a year of my life with her during holidays and work-related visits. Her presence in that house gave me the opportunity to continue to visit Winchester and the tree farmland until very recently. My uncle Bill (my mom's youngest brother) bought the original farmhouse in the mid-nineties and remodeled it into a three-story apartment. I assisted in some of that work.

A high school friend, Wayne Miller, had relocated to the Keene area (near Winchester) and I introduced him to my aunt and uncle. He has a lot of handyman builder skills, so he became quite indispensable to many projects that occurred in both those houses. His close proximity also meant we got together almost every time I was in Winchester, and this built our relationship over this lifetime. Wayne and I were very close in high school and grew closer over the years. He also became like a family member to Mimi and Bill and occasionally helps Bill with projects as Bill still lives close by.

My father's family emigrated in the early 1800's from the Alsace-Lorraine area of what was then the German Empire. They were mostly farmers and continued that tradition for several generations. They located in upstate New York west of the Adirondacks near Boonville. This picture of my great great grandfather Jacob Grubel and his 3 brothers shows a great deal of grit. It must have been a very arduous lifestyle before the advent of our oil dominated culture. I cannot even imagine cutting all the firewood by hand for a winter in upstate New York. My back hurts just thinking about it!!!

Grubel Brothers: William, Charles, Henry G., Jacob

My father's dad passed away 6 years before I was born, but his mother lived until the mid 1960's. She would cook us meals when we were visiting, though we rarely stayed overnight as she was just an hour's drive away. She was always dressed in black. This seemed odd to me. Apparently, her family custom was to mourn the death of a mate for life in that manner. We used to visit her in the home my dad grew up in until she had to be placed in a nursing home. I only visited her once there with my dad and she didn't recognize either of us. My dad's struggle with this made an impression on me. He came home from this visit and was obviously distressed. This was my first encounter with dementia that has become so prevalent in our culture now.

My first "job" for which I was paid was picking blackberries. I got 10 cents a quart and many days I could pick 10 to 15 quarts in our neighbors' blackberry patch. My first punch-the-clock job was at a place called Dairy Isle when I was 14. I got 90 cents an hour and all the mistakes I could eat! The summer after my junior year in high school I stayed with my Aunt Mimi in Winchester and worked in a tannery. My Uncle Steve was able to get me a job, as he was in charge of hiring! The A.C. Lawrence tannery in Winchester was the last remaining tannery in the US. My first two days were spent unloading sheepskins from a boxcar. The skins were packed in salt and it was incredibly hot! I lost a fingernail grabbing the skins over and over in the 105 degree heat! The regular man who did this job didn't come in those two days because of the heat. There was an expectation that I would flop the skins, spread out, onto a conveyor belt for the "trimmers" to cut off unnecessary pieces. There was extra pay for skins trimmed over a certain amount. I managed to earn us all a bit of that each day!

I soon graduated to the dye man job and was responsible for dying over 100 dozen or more sheepskins every day. The dyed water that I released went directly into the Ashuelot River. It changed color with every day. I was oblivious to the ecological damage I was participating in but eventually the EPA wasn't. The factory was forced to shut down in 1987. Part of me regrets the pollution I caused, but I must admit I really enjoyed working with the older men and made friends with several of them.

My last summer at home after I graduated high school, I got a job painting all of the elementary school classrooms with a young elementary teacher, Mr. Laurenti. I learned the skill of painting well and that later became a "trade" I mastered.

Another pathway forward in my youth involved the discovery of religion and spirituality. I was raised in a rather traditional Christian family with ties to the Presbyterian faith. The first minister I remember was a woman named Miss Chaplin (this was her name in addition to being a chaplain). She was the first woman to be called to a church in the US Presbytery. I did not realize how unique that was and I am sure she faced many obstacles along the way. I also suspect my sister Betsey acquired some inspiration from her. She was later called into that profession and became a minister in the same faith.

I found myself in my teen years interested in questions of faith and bothered by the many contradictions I experienced being displayed day to day by those who professed to be Christians. The only place I got to explore these ideas was in our youth group that was led by the only other minister I remember, Rev. Sorenson. Predestination, is there a God, what is sin, is there an afterlife and so forth we got a taste of questions many people wrestle with at some point in their lives while living in this culture. This set up a platform for me to immediately major in religion when I arrived at Earlham. This exploration of religion also made me aware of a fundamental urgency to live ethically.

The Vietnam War also played into my development as I grew up during the years it raged on. I knew while in high school I couldn't support it yet did not know how to express my opinion without seeming out of place. The war did not help my relationship with my dad. His support for the war was typical of many Americans in those days and did not change until it did for many others near the end of that failed U.S. effort.

In my late high school years, I played in a little rock band that never got anywhere. We called ourselves TeKeWaBo which was the first two letters of each of our names. The only instrument I had was a little 36-key device that claimed to be a keyboard but didn't make enough sound to complement electric guitars and drums. I didn't have enough money or knowledge about where to look for anything that might have actually made a suitable sound. I think we played one party and that was it.

The music that influenced me at the time included The Ramsey Lewis Trio, The Association (loved their harmonies), The Rolling Stones, The Beatles, classical pieces such as Pictures at an Exhibition by Mussorgrsky, Blue Danube Waltz by Strauss, Beethoven's 9th and the steady emergence of rock and roll as a preference for listening on my little radio. I also began collecting records, a few of which I still have! My parents were not exactly thrilled by my preference for rock music as it became increasingly popular and more available for listening. All of this got amplified when I got to college and discovered so much more of the great 60s music that was happening.

Discovery

My years in grade school had always been a mixed bag of emotions. I was always encouraged to excel in grades. Thankfully that was not too difficult. This emphasis or expectation led later to some forms of rebellion against the whole process. Elementary classes were mostly learning by memorization. We were encouraged to compete with each other. This may or may not have been wise, but it was a standard approach for the time. By the time high school arrived I could "succeed" but I was becoming bored with much of the material and started to care less and less if I did well. I ended up being valedictorian of my class, but it felt like a sham.

In the fall of 1968 I entered Earlham College, a Quaker college in Richmond, Indiana. I picked Earlham out of a large book that listed colleges all around the country. I applied to several other small colleges around the country and also was accepted at the Air Force Academy. How different my life would have turned out if I had gone there! I am certain going to Earlham was a huge factor in the direction my life ultimately took.

There was a significant event in that process. I was a pretty good basketball player (our high school team was 67-8 over the four years that I played) so I had been invited to play ball at Earlham. About two weeks into practice for the season the coach (Del Harris, who later coached the Houston Rockets to an NBA championship) called me into his office and asked me if I planned on cutting my hair. It wasn't that long but it was headed that way and I told him no. He told me if I didn't, I couldn't play on the team! After a half hour discussion, I left the team. I suspect that event changed the course of my life as much as any choice has. If I had continued to play ball I may have stayed the four years, and my life would look very different today. I reckon coach Harris got over his long hair thing as the NBA has been loaded with players with long hair for many years. Ces't la vie! I still love the game and played on local teams until I was in my late 50's when injuries started to take the fun out of it. I occasionally go to a local basketball court that is always open to the public. The sound of the basketball being dribbled on the hardwood floor brings up a huge sense of belonging. It is a most welcome sound and makes my whole-body smile!

My first experience of creating music got its start when I came upon a grand piano in the Quaker Meetinghouse at the college. There were many opportunities to just go there at night and play. My choice was to play with my eyes closed. I would begin by running my hands down over the keys with my foot on the sustain pedal and just sit there and

My jumpshot, felt like flying!

listen until the sound stopped. I would then let my hands do whatever came to them. This process eventually allowed me to trust music and my playing in a way I didn't learn from books or teachers. It set the stage for creating music throughout my life.

My two years at Earlham gave me the opportunity to voice my concern for the Vietnam War in a way I had not been able to at home. I went to two very large demonstrations, one in Chicago (Veterans against the war) and the other in Washington D.C. The one in Washington became a challenge as we were tear gassed and had difficulty leaving. My resolve was deepened to oppose this war and ultimately led me to seeking my CO status. Fortunately I was able to get sufficient support from several professors and friends to actually receive my Conscientious Objector status.

Thankfully that happened as I don't know what would have occurred in my life had I been cast into the military without an option. When they drew numbers for the draft, I luckily came up with number 300. It is unlikely I would have been drafted.

During my second year at Earlham I grew close to several guys in our hall. At the end of my sophomore year 5 of us dropped out together under the pretense of forming a rock band. When we left Earlham in 1970, we were fodder for the military. Fortunately, several of us got or already had CO status. What lay ahead would deepen my musical abilities and propel my life in a direction I never would have dreamed of a few short years before.

Community Evolution

Intentional Community has always played a big part in my life as an adult. The choice to live together with former classmates was a beginning and ultimately set the stage for a kind of progression that led to the purchase of Zephyr with two other families on June 25th, 1983. It was a long and winding road.

My time at Earlham ended after spring of 1970. I told my parents I was dropping out on May 1st and on May 3rd I had a different kind of encounter during a midnight swim. A group of us decided to use a pond off campus for a swim late at night. Bob Tschilske, my roommate (also fellow bandmate and now a great blues guitarist) and another friend ran off the dock ahead of me and dove in. I followed them and proceeded to find myself dangling by one leg that was stuck in a hole made by a board that was missing on the dock. It hurt like crazy yet somehow, I managed to get back to my room for the night. There was no compound fracture, but the following morning Bob had to assist me to the infirmary where I decided no doctor's visit was going to happen. I ended up on crutches for the next six weeks. While I was still at Earlham, I hung my leg in a whirlpool bath with Epsom salts three times a day. Perhaps that hastened the healing.

The crutches followed me on my journey to look for a home for the band to come to the following fall. Everyone else in the band-to-be went home for the summer, but I was not welcome home so it naturally fell to me to find a city for us to come together in. I first went to Chicago and stayed with my friend Joe Goldiamond but that visit did not yield a job or a way forward. I then hitchhiked to Boston after a few days' stay in Indiana with Chas Cole, the bass player in our band-to-be. Once in Boston, I stayed with the sister of a classmate at Earlham and within a week I had landed a job at Beth Israel Hospital as an orderly and soon after found a room on Commonwealth Ave. Two of the guys in the band came to Boston later that summer and found us the home we all moved to in September.

We occupied a large three-story house on Sheridan St. in Jamaica Plain (a Boston suburb) that had formerly been a nursing home. Only thing was, the new owner never moved the nursing home residents out before we moved in.

What a hoot! Here we are a young, energetic half crazed bunch of testosterone-driven males thrown in with 5 very old women without caregivers. We became responsible for the women, the youngest of whom was 87 (the former owner) and the oldest over 100. One of the band members, Rick, and his partner, Stephanie, inherited the job of taking care of the women and searching for other nursing homes we could move them into. They were forgotten people who had no relatives, so the job fell completely on us. The band practiced in the basement while one by one we found new homes for the ladies and ultimately by the New Year, the task was accomplished. It wasn't without some sense of loss that this occurred as we came to like these folks and I believe they were somewhat inspired by living with the young hippies as well. We even had conversations about

The house on Sheridan Street

drug use (mainly opium) with one woman who had indulged with friends in her youth before the use of drugs became illegal. All in all, not one of us would have traded this experience for anything resembling normalcy!

After the women who had lived there were relocated, we moved our instruments upstairs and began practicing in a main room on the first floor. This house was very large with three floors of living space. There was elaborate woodwork in almost every room. There was even a widows walk on the roof area. One room was designed like a ship's cabin that we turned into our smoking room complete with a great sound system and a wooden spool table covered with candles. This was my introduction to candle making which later would become part of my livelihood.

On the second floor of the house there was a bathroom that contained a 7-foot-long bathtub. What a hoot to stretch my 6 ft. 3-inch body out completely to enjoy a good soak. One evening while reading *Perelandra* by C.S. Lewis in the tub I made a conscious choice to quit smoking cigarettes. It had only been a habit for two years, but I knew it was changing my vocal abilities in a not-good way. I never smoked regularly after making that choice, though I did indulge a bit occasionally. I had a rule for myself that if I ever smoked or needed to smoke two cigarettes in a day, I would throw away whatever tobacco I had immediately. I have fortunately stuck by that rule and haven't touched it at all in over thirty years.

Sheridan Street gang, circa 1971, I'm bottom left

The band went through many name changes and eventually settled on Melted Cheese. We probably played a total of five or six gigs in that year and our repertoire was mostly cover tunes from that time. We played one original which Martin, the guitarist, wrote. I acquired a Farfisa keyboard and a Fender amp that were my introduction to electronic equipment. I also acquired an upright piano that required a gargantuan effort on the part of the guys in the band. The piano was located on the 3rd floor of an apartment building. There were three sets of stairs each turning 90 degrees and a landing between each floor. We had to actually turn the piano upside down to get it to turn the corners. It was like rolling it down the stairs. There were a few fingers and legs that met with some pain during that exercise. After all that the piano actually played pretty well for the time we shared the Sheridan St. house and then it got left behind.

The music was often loud. As a result, we were eventually asked by neighbors to stop playing by 10pm. For a period of time, we had two drummers and two keyboard players when Martin's brother Doug and his friend Muck joined us. That was a popular trend at the time, and it definitely made us louder! One night the empty house next door burned to the ground (doubtlessly set on fire by the neighborhood kids). We got to jamming and played until past midnight to accompany the firefighters and the racket going on outside. Fortunately for us, we were on great terms with the same kids, largely due to Chas, who had an affinity for the young ones! We like to think we saved the house. It is still sitting on the corner of Sheridan St. and recently sold for millions of dollars!

The band and the boys on Sheridan Street

There was a very active music scene in Boston at the time and we often took in concerts at various venues around the city. One of the best concerts I ever attended was seeing Frank Zappa and the Mothers of Invention at the Boston Tea Party. Flo and Eddie from the Turtles were singing with his incredible band and among their three encores was the pop song *Happy*

Together. Best rendition ever! I also got to see the Moody Blues, Poco, Shawn Phillips, Bo Diddley, The Flock, It's a Beautiful Day, the Mahavishnu Orchestra, RedBone, Allman Brothers, Jimi Hendrix (just before he died), Mountain, Emerson Lake and Palmer, J. Geils, ELO and many I don't remember.

The band discovered a great vocal coach, Dante Pavone. We took several lessons from him over a few months, and I know I benefited from his technique. I have always paid attention to my breathing while singing and I am sure his suggestions were part of that. Our drummer, Rick, claimed to have been damaged for life when he was asked by Dante *"What instrument do you play?"* and then after a dramatic pause dismissed with the words, *"You play drums!"* Dante was a vocal coach for performers including Paul McCartney, Mick Jagger, Aretha Franklin, and Steven Tyler. How different our lives would be if we had attained some of that kind of success!

During this time in Boston people hitchhiked everywhere. On one of my thumb-based rides I got picked up by Diana DeSimone who years later would see me off to San Francisco. She was much older than me and had seven children. Her husband had just died a few years prior while their 7th child was still in utero. The demands on her were very large and she had turned to Hatha yoga to bring some moments of relief. She invited me to attend a class in a church in Harvard Square. This class was led by a man we all knew as Yogi John who had learned from Swami Vishnudevananda. I loved the stretching and breath work and soon was attending every Tuesday for the remainder of my time in Boston. The class was also my introduction to meditation, as we would enter silence for a period at the end of every class. I became very adept at yoga and taught it in Corning NY while living at Birdsfoot Farm. Several years later I was blessed with the opportunity to attend a weekend yoga retreat with Vishnudevananda during one of my San Francisco adventures. I was the last person to enter the room when we were setting up and I ended up right in front of the Swami doing yoga for the 3-day event. He only corrected me a few times, which was encouraging and as we left the last evening, I literally fell on him wanting to give him a hug goodbye. An embarrassing moment I shall not forget. There are many postures I still rely on to stretch, and pranayama breathing is something I turn toward occasionally as well. I am ever grateful for this practice.

A band needs a vehicle to move its equipment around and somehow, I discovered a large school bus for sale that we ended up buying for that purpose. Our claim to fame was that Aerosmith borrowed the bus for a weekend when their transport broke down! Unfortunately, we ended up breaking up after a year. When we divided up our financial inputs I ended up with the bus. It was my first vehicle and not the easiest to maneuver around a big city. It took finding three parking places in a row to park, which wasn't the most convenient arrangement, so it remained parked more often than not. Ultimately the bus led to my next home!

The demise of our adventure together left us each heading in different directions. Several of us moved into apartments around Boston and others left the area for more familiar pastures. We gradually drifted apart and until the advent of the internet had little contact. This all changed in recent years as one by one we re-established our relationships. This has resulted in several reunions in recent years which I will share more about later.

I enjoyed going to live music venues and Harvard Square was one of the best at that time. One Sunday in early August of 1971, a band called Spirit in Flesh was playing on the square. The band was from an intentional community called The Brotherhood of Spirit. A large number of members of the community were there in attendance, having hitchhiked to the concert. I ended up talking with several people and offered my bus as a ride back to the community. That trip resulted in me joining the community and giving them the bus. There were about 300 people, 95 % young adults living with minimal money but somehow functioning with many stated ideals that translated into a mostly positive experience for me. There were no rules other than no alcohol, no drugs, and no premarital sex and if you had a problem with someone you went to work it out immediately. I honestly never saw drugs or alcohol while there and have no way of knowing about the rest.

Though it was not a final destination (is there one?), my time there heightened in me a desire to live with others in an intentional community. I also found myself in confusion about the hierarchy I saw developing in the community. This ultimately caused me to question my value to myself or others while there. I left on Christmas day by walking to my grandfather's home where my aunt Mimi lived. It was only four miles away. My parents happened to be there. We talked, I asked for 10 dollars and hitchhiked back to Boston to resume my time there until spring. The bus stayed behind to become the publicity bus for the band Spirit in Flesh. Upon return to Boston I shared an apartment on Queensberry St. with my high school friend Lou, her husband and their child. I was lucky and got a job in the parking lot at the hospital. In the spring of 1972, I hitchhiked to northern California where I landed on a mountaintop in Mendocino County.

California Beckons

Part of this hitchhiking journey was an extended stay in Marquette, Michigan. Phil Powell, (an Earlham friend whose place I was headed for) asked me to accompany two young women the rest of the way on my hitchhike. They were not ready to leave when I arrived in Marquette, so I lingered there for two weeks. This happened to be around early June and it was during the time when the ice broke on Lake Superior. The local ritual was to jump in the lake when the ice broke. I didn't participate but I watched a bunch of folks do the deed! I was amazed at their enthusiasm! With the sun shining off the big ice chunks, seeing people in the water was quite the sight. Shortly after we left just as the mosquitoes arrived en masse. It turned out to be a good thing I waited for those ladies as one of them later married Phil. They eventually had two children together.

I am not sure how I got by during this trip to California. Phil owned 70 acres on a gorgeous mountain top in Mendocino County. There was only one structure, and it was open to the elements. We had to walk down his 2-mile drive to the South Fork Eel River to bathe and there certainly was no electricity up on the ridge top. I didn't have a job, nor was there any prospect of securing one. Branscomb was the town we were near. It consisted of a post office, a small general store and a lumber mill.

I got to fight one forest fire while I was there. Someone handed me a 5-gallon bucket of water and a towel and instructed me to beat at the grassy areas where the fire was moving forward with the wet towel. I did this for 5 hours and it was amazingly effective. With water being limited, I got far more accomplished with that towel and bucket than could be done with a hose. Later in my life, I was able to save a house from an approaching fire with this technique.

The area near Branscomb was covered with large redwood trees as far as the eye could see. This provided me with an experience I have never forgotten, getting lost in the woods. There were few neighbors, and they were not close by. One day we were invited to a party a few miles away by car. Soon after arriving I realized I really wasn't into being there. I then set out in the woods in the direction of Phil's land, thinking I could find my way back. This was a very foolish idea! As I rambled along, each ridgetop became just like the last one and by sundown I knew I was really lost. I had been trying to follow a direction by the sun's position and now that was gone. Fortunately, it was a full moon so I had some light to maneuver under. There was little undergrowth as the trees were very tall, so walking was fairly easy. Then a minor miracle occurred. I crossed an old logging trail on a ridge top and I knew that a logging trail had been near Phil's land. After about 45 minutes of following that trail, I came to what was a recognizable path and soon after was home. My relief was palatable. This adventure wasn't a planned one but certainly was a challenging, eye-opening moment in my life.

The ocean was 10 miles to the west as the crow flies. During sunsets when the fog wasn't blocking our view, I could see bits of reflection of the sun's light as it set over the ocean. Several times I was lucky to see a green flash as the sunset. I later learned there are many who seek to see that flash, as it is a relatively rare occurrence.

Near the end of my time for this California excursion I pulled out my guitar and a song burst through titled *I Love You Friend*. It was a *thank you* to Phil for sharing his beautiful place with me that summer. I had made many attempts at songwriting before that moment. This is the first one that stuck. It became a theme song for me during my twenties and ended up on my first recording years later.

I Love You Friend

Well I traveled far to greet you
I was guided by a light to this place
The hills are so green you know what I mean
In a world that's a miracle to call your home

We are one and the truth of that will soon be shown
There's a light shining in your eyes.
And I love you friend, this ain't the end.

There are many ways of growing. Just be sure to say amen
Cause the force is so strong it'll take you along
Under a sun that gives life to everyone
Plant your seeds watch the miracle of new life begun
There's a light shining in your eyes
And I love you friend, this ain't the end.

My newfound idealism shines through this song and so does the Force many years before the Star Wars movies! Alas, I had to return to the east coast.

My hitchhike back to Boston contained several surprises. My first ride was with a couple, Richard Allen and his then musician wife, Kris. They made candles for a living at the time and invited me to spend the night with them, which I gratefully accepted. The next morning, they got out their wax and went to it. I already had an interest in candle making from my days making candles for the band's "spool candle table". Witnessing their process inspired me and eventually I asked them if they would mind if I tried to make the candles back east. In response, they said go for it!

Back in Boston again, I shared another apartment in the same building as Lou with other friends. I found a wax supplier and figured out the process of making some very attractive candles. I next, somehow, ended up at a craft fair on Harvard Sq. where the candles sold like hot cakes. I made enough money to purchase my first of several VW bugs and engineer my next escape to the country.

Sabbath was the child of my friends whose apartment I shared upon my return to Boston. Her mom was a tall Jewish woman from Newton, MA and her dad was a short intense black man from Jamaica with a huge afro. Their baby was beautiful! I would love to see her now! This song came in her honor while living a few months with them on Queensbury St.

A Child Was Born

A child was born to some friends not long ago
And I'm a wondering why she's her and how she's gonna grow
In a world that seems so far away from her eyes. From her eyes
There's paradise there and everywhere in her sight
You cry so loud and stir the night
Nothing goes unanswered smiles surround your sight
The way you are greeted like a dawning light
There's paradise there and everywhere in her sight.

And so young one you will learn to change in love and pain
I wish for you a life of calm, sweet peace within
And further on amidst the dawn that we might see the sun
There's paradise there and everywhere in everyone… a child was born.

The return trip to Boston also provided me with a new destination in the country as well as the means to get there. During that journey I spent a brief time in San Francisco. To find a way back home I checked out a bulletin board offering ride sharing. This ultimately connected me with a fellow driving a big, old early 50's Buick and it connected me with Katie. She shared the ride to Chicago and told me about her sister who lived with a man on a farm in upstate New York who needed someone to take care of his farm, as he was planning to leave the farm soon. I connected with Bruce,. the owner of Birdsfoot Farm. We hit it off and soon the farm became my home for most of the next three years. I shared the first year there with Katie who joined me there a few months after I arrived.

My early 20s then became a process of discovery that focused on country living skills, relationship building and steering my life toward a path that I believed would give me a measure of freedom to explore myself and what it might be I was here to accomplish. I somehow survived with very little money, lots of friends, some music and a passion to live as simply as possible in the country.

Lessons Learned

I grew up in upstate New York in a small town and I now found myself 22 years later living on a farm in the southern tier of New York State near another small town called Addison, close to Corning. Surrounded by elderly neighbors and 400 acres of beautiful land, this place would be my first real learning ground for country life.

I am much indebted to Marjorie and Ralph Northrup as they adopted me as a second son. Ralph got me onto his tractors, building fences and taking part in other farm chores. This was an introduction to skills I would use for the rest of my life. I had to learn to cut wood, grow a garden, can food, make cheese from the milk of goats Katie and I acquired among many other skills that became lifelong essentials to living in the woods!

I shared the home with several friends, particularly Paul R. (who perished in a fire at the age of 45), Bill Deats, an emerging and still active artist, and a couple who had a child while living with me there. Paul played drums, which were always set up in the living room. We cranked up the music to dance and celebrate our time together. Katie left after a year but in her time there she introduced me to EST (Erhard Seminar Training). I took the training at the Commodore Hotel in Central Square In New York City. I am grateful for the eye-opening challenges that Werner Erhard laid down in front of me and 200 other people, including John Denver and his mother during this training.

There were two times while I was responsible for the farm that I left with thoughts of starting a different path forward. The first occurrence is one that I am not too proud of. I celebrated the last day of the last job I ever punched a clock on by going to a bar with the intent of picking up a woman. This was a first for me and fortunately or unfortunately, it worked. There was a piano in the bar and as I was playing Gloria walked up and ended up coming home with me. The night before this happened, all the folks I lived with at Birdsfoot and some visitors were dancing together to the song Gloria and we ended up in a pile on the floor. I think I took that as a good omen. She became a part of my life for the next several months. Most of it was fine but she had an alcohol problem I had no understanding of or experience with. She was 10 years older than me and lived a very different lifestyle. In my naiveté, I thought going to California would give her a chance to start over. This was an early lesson in the misplaced energy of fixing or rescuing someone.

We took to the road in my 63 Ford Galaxy to start a life in California and it lasted one days' journey. Our first stop was in Erie PA with my lifelong friend Lou, who then lived in Erie. Gloria asked me to get her flask out of the car. I refused and what ensued was a confrontation that was not pretty, to say the least. Gloria came after me with a fork and some dark intent! Lou managed to keep us separate enough for no damage to be done! Gloria was fetched back to Corning late that night and the next day I continued on my way to California to remain there for only a month. A few years later I discovered Gloria had cancer. I was able to contact her and we had a good and forgiving conversation. She died several years later while only in her early forties.

I struggled to find work on this journey and often wondered why I was in California. The straw that broke the camel's back on that trip was losing my dog Mindy during a concert in Golden Gate Park. I was doubtless stoned, and I entered the concert with her following me at my feet. She was not on a leash. My mistake!   Soon in the enormous crowd, I could not locate her. I spent the rest of the afternoon trying to find her and returned to my room without her that night. I was despondent! The next morning, I called the SPCA and lo and behold a man had just brought her in. She did have tags and she had taken up with his dog on a walk that morning. I had to bail her out with my last 5 dollars. I borrowed some money from a friend and left for the farm back East later that day. I returned to the farm somewhat humbled and with a lifelong distaste for alcohol consumption in any quantity. Mindy and I remained together until 1987 when she passed away here where I live now. She was an awesome companion through many changes in my life!

The second time was a second attempt in college at Earlham. A fellow showed up at the farm in early August of 1974 who was driving to Richmond, Indiana and on a whim, I went with him to see if I could get back into Earlham. In one day, I got accepted, got a job working in the library and found a room to rent in a house with other off-campus students. I wasn't sure what to make of it, but it happened so fast I figured this was what I needed to do. I turned the farm over to Paul and company and headed back to school. It didn't take long to recall that I was no longer motivated by this kind of learning. My ground of being had shifted so much I just couldn't relate to a lot of what was being offered. By halfway through the semester, I knew I was going to be dropping out again. I aced the two classes I remained in and I headed back to the farm.

While living at Birdsfoot Farm I managed to acquire an old upright piano. I resumed my routine of playing with my eyes closed after stroking the entire keyboard. During one of those episodes my first song on piano appeared. It is called the Treasure and contains an ode to Shakespeare. There is a quote from *The Merchant of Venice* that I worked into the refrain. "The quality of mercy is not strained. It droppeth like a gentle rain upon the place beneath." I still play the song occasionally. I titled my first recording, released in 1987 many years later, *Treasures in the Stream*. The title of the recording was a clear metaphor for how I was receiving the songs over time.

The Treasure

Can't ignore it or explore it must be somewhere in between
Glad I found it, I'd resound it, if I knew what it should mean
Yes these thoughts they still come round for me
As I welcome my freedom patiently
The quality of mercy is not strained
It droppeth like a gentle rain upon the place beneath

Some search madly. Others sadly sink right out of view
In this short race I'm sure there's enough space to get us all through
Yes these thoughts etc.

There's a treasure without measure and lies within me and you
You can find it, in fact you got it and there's nothing else you can do
Yes these thoughts etc.

I picked up a little guitar while playing with the band in Boston. This eventually served me well while in future bands. I could look at the guitarist and get a clue where we were going key-wise. I never mastered much more than playing pretty solid rhythm guitar and some finger picking but that proved to be a good foundation. I had an acoustic guitar and I acquired an electric guitar that I loved to play! It was a white body Fender telecaster. It yielded the song *Jumping Up and Down Together* while I lived on the farm. Later it became necessary to sell the guitar when my life got stripped down to all I could hold on my back. I wonder how much more guitar I would be playing if I still had possession of that guitar. This song made it onto my second album recording, *Circles Returning*.

Jumping Up and Down Together

You better start looking at what went on before
Cause just up ahead you're still knocking your head on that door
Believe in the sky, wondering why
Crazy blue patches gonna open your eyes
And we're still jumping up and down together, jumping up and down together, jumping up and down together, why don't we start now?

The Buddha's bizarre we're still driving all these cars how's the weather?
You come from your heart and get a new start it's getting better
Believe in the crop it'll never go flop
If we're planting our seeds, we might never stop
Jumping up and down together, jumping up and down together, jumping up and down together, why don't we start now?

Bundles of green will not clean your machine just surrender
When you're on a good track and you must circle back ah remember
Sometimes you're hot and sometimes you're cold
The idea is not that you are what you're told
And we're still jumping up and down together, jumping up and down together
Jumping up and down together, why don't we start now?

A big part of this period of my life was my absorbing many different ideas about how to be here in this world. Books like *Be Here Now*, *The Fourth Way*, *Programming and Metaprogramming in the Human Biocomputer*, *Zen and the Art of Motorcycle Maintenance*, *The Tao Te Ching*, *The I Ching*, *Autobiography of a Yogi*, *The Nature of Personal Reality* and many others contributed to shifting a ground of being for me that persists to this day. All of this was enhanced by the conversations that ensued with the folks I lived with both on the farm and in a larger community that was evolving around me at the time. This learning also emerged in my songwriting as the years ahead rolled by.

The end of my time on Birdsfoot Farm arrived with Bruce's desire to sell the farm. I unloaded everything I had except for a pickup truck, my dog and her puppies and headed back to Boston. I parked my dog Mindy, her offspring Chia, and Chia's seven pups with my Aunt Mimi in New Hampshire. I owe her eternal gratitude for accepting responsibility for those many dogs. She had to take the pups and Chia to a pound and upon my return from this California trip I retrieved Mindy.

Mindy and I at Earlham

I then went to Boston and sold the truck to the son of Diana DeSimone (my friend whom I briefly stayed with in Newton, Massachusetts) and bought a plane ticket to San Francisco. Now I am reduced to the clothes on my back and a suitcase. With a slight sense of trepidation and a great deal of anticipation I am on my way west once again.

Upon arrival on the west coast, I stayed with a friend, Lynn Bell, whom I met at Earlham during my second attempt at higher learning. Lynn had come out as gay and was attempting to seduce me the night I arrived. Fortunately for me, that just didn't go with my vibe. I feel lucky I didn't waiver in my choice to be heterosexual as HIV was perched just around the corner for so many folks I encountered during that stay. Many of my friends were gay, and though I wasn't gay I enjoyed their company and their relaxed way of being.

During this six-month stint in San Francisco, I didn't get the opportunity to play much music. I did acquire a Fender Rhodes keyboard, but really didn't have enough skill to carry myself into gigs, solo or otherwise. For part of this time I lived in an apartment at the end of Golden Gate Park. I roamed in the park often. It was a taste of the country that I craved! Later I shared an apartment with a friend of Katie's who lived 2 blocks from the SanFrancisco Bay. She and I took the EST training together many years earlier . She now worked for EST and made a very good salary. I was able to live there for 50 bucks a month by being her valet, doing her laundry, and keeping the place stocked in food. I occupied a very large room with glass windows that looked out over the city. After the 1989 earthquake I happened to be watching "the news" and saw someone go into that apartment and interview the current residents. It was nearly destroyed and a grocery store I frequented nearby had burned to the ground. I never experienced an earthquake during my California adventures and I have to say I am very glad of that!

One main benefit of this trip was being given the chance to learn deep tissue massage at the International Center for Release and Integration, run by Jack Painter. He developed Postural Integration. It was akin to Rolfing (Structural Integration) that he and Ida Rolfe developed together. The difference was Jack remained very open to and encouraging of practitioners to include whatever skills beside Rolfing they acquired along the way in their practice. I was able to trade my painting and fix-it skills to attend the class and get my certification. It was many years later that I realized I had been thrown into the leading edge of massage work. The skills I learned would be decades making their way into massage schools across the country. I retained my massage license until recently, but never did it full time. I just added it to my bag of tricks to get by! I remain grateful for the knowledge about the bodymind I was gifted so early in my life.

Another gift of this time in San Francisco was my introduction to Tai Chi as taught by Benjamin Lo in the lineage of Cheng Man Ching. This 37-movement form would open me to awareness of the subtle ways energy moves in the body. I have found the practice to be very rewarding. I have been blessed to encounter the same form being taught three times in my life, most recently about 15 years ago at the Chinese Clinic here in Floyd. While I do not practice every day currently, I do occasionally enter into the form as I remember it. Just doing a small amount brings a sense of presence and wellbeing that is very beneficial. Occasionally I will look up a video of Benjamin performing the form and practice along. For me, this is one of the blessings of the current internet.

On my 26th birthday (Feb 28, 1976) I made this entry into my journal.

"I am trying (every time I use this word, I feel like I am lying) to create a future course that will benefit me in being the way to a home and the way to my heart. I now know I could be serving people by living in a city and doing P.I. and I also could learn more bodywork stuff. This is attractive to me except I do not care for city life that much. I want very much to be in the country somewhere, making this creation of mine with other folks of like yearning and creativity. Places I could go! Hubbard Hill, Sunrise farm, anywhere in Steuben County, Amherst, Portland Maine, Brattleboro, Keene N.H area, Virginia."

This turned out to be very prophetic, particularly regarding Virginia, which I had never been to or knew anyone who lived there at the time.

Calling Calling

In early April of 1976 I got the message (from guides or whatever it is that we sense leads us sometimes in life) to return to the east coast because I would meet the woman who I was going to have children with. Three days later I headed onto the road again with my thumb and I returned to live with friends I made while at Birdsfoot Farm in Steuben County. Shortly after my return I decided to visit a commune called Hubbard Hill which was near Ithaca NY. I had made friends there while selling candles at a few craft fairs in years past. I met a woman there named Jayn Avery and we soon took up with each other. By July, I had moved in with her in her very primitive little round house.

Hubbard Hill, winter of 1977

The community of Hubbard Hill consisted of artisans and craftsmen and was based on a lot of ideals that actually worked for this group. Our money was not personal, everyone shared our vehicles, and the food and expenses were shared by everyone as well. There were only eight of us with a few changes in the year and half while I was there, but it basically worked. I existed in a quiet optimism throughout this time while sharing an ideal lifestyle I was immersed in. The land was beautiful, and this added to our shared experience. We called our pottery Blue Heron Pottery because most evenings in the summer months we could see blue herons in flight returning to their rookery which happened to be on our land.

A few months after we got together at Hubbard Hill we attended the Rhinebeck craft fair which was a big show at that time. As we walked toward the exit I glanced over at a truck sitting in line to leave and saw Claire (my first lover) sitting there with her pottery partner Dave. Jayn and I ran over and sat in the truck with them for a brief acquaintance and sharing update! I felt this affirmation of my course in life as I sat there with my first lover and the woman I was now creating my life with. It was as if some kind of magic circle was blessing me.

Jayn and I knew right away we wanted to have children and by November we were pregnant. Our first daughter, Amy Sunshine, was born on July 19, 1977, after a very long labor. Though we wanted a home birth, we ended up in the hospital where she arrived within an hour after we checked in. We checked out 45 minutes later. One of my strongest memories of living this life is sitting on our little porch holding Amy on my forearm (her whole body fit on my arm, yipes!) and just feeling overwhelmed and grateful at the same time!

I admit I had no idea what lay ahead, but I felt Jayn and I could handle whatever came our way. The rest of the year was hard but good. Jayn was a developing potter when we met, and I joined the

Baby Amy, day 1

trade. We made pottery together for the next 18 years and basically provided for our family from that skill. It is still Blue Heron Pottery to this day, under Jayn's steady, creative hands. My musical path was largely sidelined at Hubbard Hill. I played my acoustic guitar a wee bit. There was no piano available, but the music did not disappear.

1977 was a year of beginnings and endings in my life. My father died, my sister Betsey got married, Amy was born and in the fall my grandfather, Guy (my moms' dad), died as well. Jayn and I held a celebration for Amy's arrival in the fall that my mom and sisters attended. I wrote a song that expressed those changes. *Inside Outside* never got recorded but I did play it a lot at gatherings in the years going forward. Recently, I played it at a memorial ceremony for a friend. It was the first time I had picked up a guitar in years.

Inside Outside

Inside outside which way are you going?
Up down all 'round look at how we're growing
    Unity of heart and mind
    The quality of life defined
    By health and happiness we share
    The hope of all to make it here

And in the end we've done our best
To make this life a joyful quest

Inside outside which way are you going?
Up down all 'round look at how she's growing
　She don't ask for nothing much
　But love and understanding touch
　Sheltered place into the night
　Warm embrace to ease her fright
　Poets hearts have searched the skies
　To know the things within her eyes

Inside outside which way are you going?
Up down all 'round look at how he's growing
　Out into the universe
　To merge with things of countless verse
　Spiraling out through spreading light
　No body left to hinder flight
　Suffering is all despair
　I thank you for your love and care

Inside outside which way are you going?
Up down all 'round look at how we're growing

Another feature of my life at Hubbard Hill was my renewed commitment to keeping goats that I had started while at Birdsfoot farm. I built a small barn and fences necessary to keep them in. Thus we had milk for our daughter Amy. Goats became a part of my life for most of the next 20 plus years.

I enjoyed their company and the caregiving fit in with my country lifestyle. Their manure fed our gardens, and their milk and cheese fed our bodies. I also understood that their milk was closer to human milk in quality and thus better for children than cows' milk. I made a lot of goat cheese and yogurt over the years. This commitment to keeping goats and gardens also tied me to wherever I was living in a manner that made taking to the road for any extended period impossible. Again, touring has never really entered my mind as a possibility given my lifestyle choices.

Amy on left, Dolphin on right, goats all around us, circa 1989.

The end of Hubbard Hill came somewhat dramatically when Peter (the owner of the property and a member of the community) decided he needed to sell and move on with his life. What ensued, though, was a testament to faith in the good intentions of people. Jayn and I had just dropped $1800 into the communal pot two weeks before this change was announced, and it was all gone so we had nothing. We had no car, no place to live and a five-month-old child. Within weeks we found a friend with a few rooms to rent in a farmhouse near Interlaken on the other side of Ithaca. She also was a potter and allowed us access to her kilns which was a great help going forward. We then created a caravan of vans and trucks to help us move around January 3rd or so. This move involved seven goats, their hay, many large truckloads of wood and our meager belongings. Within a week the snow started up and we were in a long winter whiteout until almost June. The most severe winter I can ever remember.

This is the juncture at which my mom came in to assist us as well. She gave us $500 which enabled me to find a Chevy SuperSport car that, with the back seat removed and a roof rack, we could do craft shows. Jayn could also get to her job in Binghamton teaching pottery. Somehow, we made it until spring and a craft show in Washington, D.C. It was from this show that we had decided we would try to visit southwest Virginia and look into a county named Floyd. We had heard from friends that Floyd was a great place to live the lifestyle we desired. It was also further south and could provide a longer growing season for our gardens. Luck was with us when we met a woman at the show in D.C. who offered us a place to stay near Floyd while we looked for a home connection. We made the trip, and though Floyd didn't answer the bell at that time, Pud Blair did.

We were disappointed that nothing manifested in Floyd, but our friend mentioned that she had heard of a man who had a cabin to rent near Wytheville, VA, and that he might have an opening for someone seeking to rent. When we left on our return trip to upstate New York we found the cabin, but it was obviously being lived in. Continuing down the dirt road I saw a farmer on his tractor in his barnyard and figured this might be Pud. I approached him and a 45-minute conversation ensued which led to him offering us the house he was born in. We took a walk through his empty cornfields, found the house, walked the ½ mile drive and considered this as a possibility. The house had electricity but no running water, just a spring box at the bottom of a hill 40 yards from the house.

Upon returning to continue the conversation with Pud, he offered us the house. The terms were rent free for as long as we would like if I could fix a portion of the house that had a crumbling foundation. I had helped a friend from my Birdsfoot days to move his small house by jacking it up onto a lowboy trailer so I figured I could jack this framed building up and rebuild the foundation under it. When the time came to tackle the task, I also had ample help from my Uncle Bill who has been like a brother to me and will time and again show up as an assistant for my life projects. A deal was struck with Pud . As we drove away that day, we both remarked how crazy it seemed that we would be moving in a short time into a place where we knew no one. We were operating on some kind of faith, and it seemed like the logical next step for us. We moved about six weeks later. This became our home for the next two-plus years, and music reentered my life with the arrival of an old upright piano.

One day I was sitting at the piano when Amy crawled up in my lap. I crossed my hands to hold her there and this funky thing started to happen. Soon after some lyrics arrived and the song *We Live Inside A Body* was born. This song became part of my repertoire for many decades and pops up once in a while still.

We Live Inside A Body

I live inside a body, it's made of clay
And just like clay it changes
It's a different thing each day.
In that body, all of humanity, in that body

Each molecule's a firmament revolving within us
Sowing messages of life
Learn to love yourself
In that body, feed it well, in that body

Suffering comes often, we know it through and through
A joyful climb just seems to rhyme
With being here with you
In that body oh how fine to be in that body

This is the only song I have released three times. Once on *Treasures in the Stream*, again on the first Grace Note album, *I Always Dreamed of Flying*, with a live version and finally an updated version on *Rewind*.

The second verse reflects what would become a lifelong desire to become in touch with what my body needed in terms of nourishment. This means both physical understanding of what good food could provide and a literal sensing in-to what messages I give my body by the thoughts I entertain. Also, an awareness of what my body is telling me its needs for a balanced, thriving existence. In line with the providing of good food I became a devoted organic gardener, starting with my time at Birdsfoot farm and continuing throughout my entire life until now. I learned to grow fresh vegetables all year round and canned and stored food as necessary. I also became a fan of organic fruit and maintain an orchard with apples, pears and cherries as well as raise blueberries, raspberries, and figs.

There is something beyond words that occurs for me while tending a garden. Perhaps it is the most prominent relationship I have been blessed to have with the earth itself. What I receive in the form of sustenance reminds me daily of the gift of life I have been given from the very substance of this earth. The maintenance of a garden or orchard in all the seasons requires almost daily presence and I have been fortunate to share that responsibility with like-minded partners or friends all my life. This is another big reason why touring just never called out to me.

Our time in the Wytheville area was productive in many ways. It got an immediate boost when Peter sold Hubbard Hill. He had agreed to provide everyone who lived at Hubbard Hill a sort of pension for every three months they lived there. Ours totaled the 1800 we had left in the pot just prior to learning we needed to move. This little windfall came just in time to purchase a pickup truck that led to finding clay we ended up digging and using for 10 years. The farmer who sold us the truck mentioned that pottery had been made on his land in the 1800's and he showed us some shards from pots he had found. He then led us to a place in a field where he said there was lots of clay. He moved a long stick that sat in a hole in the ground and the clay just bubbled up for the taking. We extracted more than 10,000lbs over the next decade until my back just couldn't do it anymore.

Pouring freshly screened clay for drying, circa 1981

I also built a woodfire kiln and became proficient at firing it both in Wytheville and again in Floyd when we finally landed there. There are very few people who have cut as much firewood as I have in this life. I continue to this day to heat my house with wood and love the process of gathering it from the woods.

Our daughter, Amy Sunshine, whom we often referred to as Boo, grew into a child with great curiosity, which always kept us on our toes. On May 16, 1980, she was joined by her sister Dolphin Moon.

Dolphin's arrival was quite unexpected. The morning of her birth Jayn had carried some 5-gallon buckets of water up the hill from the spring and she started bleeding. This was also the day our midwives were coming to visit us for the first time from Floyd. When Catherine and Pat arrived at 2:00 pm it didn't take long for them to pronounce that Jayn was in fact in labor. Ouch and wow!!! We thought we were in month seven, so we were totally unprepared for this. We dropped Amy at a friends' home in Pulaski on the way to the hospital. At 9:52 pm Dolphin joined our little family (this is the same exact time I entered the earthly realm many years before). I remained at the hospital for only a brief time and then returned to our home where I cleaned up and arranged life to accommodate our new

Building my first woodfire kiln, circa 1978

Baby Dolphin, home from the hospital

arrival. I also remember watching the last game of the finals in the NBA playoffs that year featuring the 76ers and Lakers. Basketball was a big part of my life for many years as I grew up. It was a more than welcome diversion for me then as I dealt with this new reality. I was a little scared and very excited, it was like the tipoff to a new ball game. The game didn't start until 11pm and I was cleaning until 2am that night.

During these 2 years in Wytheville, we were often visiting Floyd—about an hour away—cultivating our friendships there and hoping for an opening to actually make a move. There were few like-minded individuals where we were living, but there were many people we were drawn to in Floyd. Our landlords, Pud and Marge, were awesome, very kind and generous with us. The fact I did indeed fix the house to maintain its viability as a living space kept our rent at zero and I think enamored Pud to us. I also know he really enjoyed seeing Amy and perhaps thought of us as family. I revisited them in 2004 and their son Jeff, who was 15-17 at the time we lived there, had taken up residence in the house we saved and turned it into a more modern home. In my life there is often something hidden in the current moment that unfolds in the years ahead like a seed that blooms forth providing for future generations.

We now had our hands full and though I had a piano and a guitar, music wasn't a high priority unless I played for the pure pleasure of it. A few songs did arrive in those moments in Wytheville when I sat to play. *Strong Foundation* echoed the desire for a more settled situation than we found ourselves in.

Strong Foundation

Build yourself a strong foundation like deep roots in the ground
Know yourself and where you are going, and the clouds won't bring you down
The living is easy when the river runs freely
In the direction you're going can you shine on patiently?

And if you worry, you're not alone, there's a dark side to us all
In the beginning, the middle and end so many openings in the walls
The giving is easy when the doors open wide
If you step through the shadows, can you shine on quietly?
And if you need friendship or a roof o'er your head

Just turn your heart to the sun
But if you need guidance in choosing your way
Times of deliverance are times you must say

I'll build myself a strong foundation like deep roots in the ground
I'll know myself and where I am going, and the clouds won't bring me down.

Another song from this era is *Freedom Eyes*. This became a favorite to play during the Grace Note years. The lyrics reflect the recognition that something bigger than Self existed in my life and this world. I always love singing this song with others, as the refrain yields itself to quick learning, great harmonies, and a lyric that seemed to inspire audiences.

Freedom Eyes

In this age we will be wiser, in this time we all will know
On this day we can have vision and everything will shine
In our hearts there will be radiance, in our souls there shall be peace
On our lips the words will form to give our inner thoughts release

Freedom growing like a sunrise, wisdom nurtured in our eyes
We must dare to see each other, neighbors, friends, all humankind!

And the other creatures with us, take their breaths the same as we
Though their words remain as soundings they can teach us how to be
From the snowflakes on the mountains to the mists upon the seas
There is life within the rivers flowing inside you and me

Freedom growing like a sunrise, wisdom nurtured in our eyes
We must dare to see each other, neighbors, friends, all humankind!

In the morning when you rise up feel your dreams return to you
Imagine that your life is perfect, and you'll love the view
And if you hear the children laughing remember why they came to you
And if there is no one beside you the light still shines within for you
Freedom growing like a sunrise, wisdom nurtured in our eyes
We must dare to see each other, neighbors, friends, all humankind!

Arrival at Zephyr

During the summer of 1980, Jayn and I made our connection with living in Floyd. Friends whom we had made during the previous two years were leaving their rental farmhouse to move onto land they had recently acquired. We were able to meet the owners and make an agreement that would shepherd us to our new home. This place was named Zephyr and it would become the community I so desired to live in and share as the future unfolded.

On September 15, 1980, we landed at Zephyr in Floyd with two kids, a pregnant goat, our belongings and much enthusiasm for a new beginning. For me, this was also a culmination of a many years' quest. Much like the move from Hubbard Hill, we were graced with the assistance of several families and individuals who formed another caravan of vehicles to make the move happen. The day closed out with a potluck supper, the first of hundreds in the following years. The next morning when I visited the small barn I had built that summer, there stood two baby goats (both does) next to their mother. I suspected this place would be fertile ground and this was only the beginning in so many ways.

The original Zephyr homestead, circa 1980

The house was located just five miles from the town of Floyd and within a mile of the Blue Ridge Parkway. It lacked running water and electricity but had a nice spring right behind it with a spring box that was developed by the owners. We had plenty of experience living this simply and felt right at home almost immediately. There were propane lights and a propane cook stove. We also had a Home Comfort wood cook stove which somehow had followed me from the days of Birdsfoot Farm. Big skylights were a favorite feature with a starry nighttime view that often accompanied our drifting to sleep. The house was insulated, which was a step up from some places in the past. Built in 1929 by a neighbors' family, it was very rustic and very much home. Our joy at arriving in Floyd was matched by the beauty of the land and the prospect of a home to put roots down in.

The next two months were some of the "busiest" days of my life. I converted a back porch area into a studio for us to make our pottery. I also rebuilt our wood fire kiln and added on to the barn for the goats and chickens. We inherited a garden space that had been tended for many years. It was a gift that caught our attention because we wouldn't have to start from scratch with the garden. By the completion of the Christmas season, Jayn and I were settled in and no doubt counting our many blessings.

During the 1980's there were many gatherings in the alternative communities of Floyd. These times provided opportunities to share food, laughter, song, ceremony and the many visions we all were creating of how to manifest our lives. It was at one such gathering at Riverflow (another intentional community) where we met Katherine and Ray Chantal, and Tom Franko. The five of us were sitting together and felt an immediate ease and flow with each other. Through the next few years our relationships evolved through shared conversations and activities. The five of us eventually decided to look for land to live on and began the process of searching for a "home" together. We had all lived in intentional communities before and this heightened our resolve to be together in such a way.

Throughout the 70s I had moved around a lot. The 80s and onward would prove to be very different. I had been in an intentional community three times including the band house in Boston, The Brotherhood of Spirit and then Hubbard Hill. In late 1982 the farm Jayn and I rented, Zephyr, became available for purchase and we (myself, Jayn, Katherine, Ray and Tom) made an offer. It was rejected and we kept looking elsewhere. Then in spring of 1983 the owners contacted us again and we reached an agreement for the purchase of Zephyr.

With the purchase of Zephyr, Jayn and I and the kids settled into our lives shared with others in a way that really felt blessed. When you live in the country, often finding other children to play with your kids requires lots of transportation and planning. But we were lucky to have the Chantal boys around and occasionally Tom and his girls. Our first summer here Ray Chantal built a large platform with a tepee and small cooking facility for his family. They lived there all summer and fall. By the time cold weather hit Ray and the community at large had built a small house as a beginning home for their family. It has expanded over the years and is the first place anyone sees when entering Zephyr. It took a few years for other homes to be built and by 1985-6 we were all living on the farm full-time. The Giesslers joined us in 1987-88 and built a large log cabin by the early 90's. By then we were 4 households sharing the land and our lives.

As our time together unfolded, we realized we wanted to hold the land in a different manner than was usual for the time then called tenants in common. We did a lot of research into land trusts, hired a lawyer and eventually over the course of several years and countless conversations completed a document that laid out the Zephyr Land Trust. This allowed us to be beneficiaries to the trust but in fact we don't own the land. We were able to work through the complicated process of selling a home and welcoming new members to the community when the Giesslers sold their house and moved to town around 2014. Perrin and Jenny Heartway and their children joined Zephyr then and have added a youthful presence to our community. At this time, we have been five households since 1994 when Jayn and I got divorced and I began building my own home here that I remain in today.

The Choice–Rise Up Singing is a song that came through sometime early in my years at Zephyr. It shares a metaphorical question that still remains unanswered. Will we rise up singing in the sun or will we leave our work undone? The song has a large vocal finish that I have been lucky to perform with church choirs. It has given me chills more than once to hear. This song is one of my favorites!

The Choice-Rise Up Singing

Please forgive me when I raise my voice
I do not mean you harm, I am dying to know you
In relations when I make the choice to reach out once again
To be happy, to be anything at all
Will we rise up singing in the sun or will we leave our work undone?

Are we children caught up in our games
Smothered by our names for each other what a silly way to go
On this journey the challenge is so great
It's hard to contemplate where we're going when it's all right here
Will we rise up singing in the sun or will we leave our work undone?

Rise, rise up singing. Rise, rise up singing.
Will we rise up singing in the sun or will we leave our work undone?

Education of our youth was also on all our minds. Together with several other like-minded families from other areas in Floyd County we started an alternative school that became Blue Mountain School. It began as a Waldorf school and during my participation it was primarily a parent run cooperative. Both my daughters, Amy and Dolphin, attended Blue Mountain through the 7th grade. Currently my granddaughter Pearl and three of the Heartway children are attending the school. Jenny Heartway has been a teacher there since they arrived at Zephyr. She has represented Zephyr's continued involvement with Blue Mountain School and its evolution.

It was for the school that the next bands I played with were formed as we played fundraisers for the school throughout the 80's and early 90's. A six- or seven-piece band we named Just Jake played often in town to enthusiastic dance crowds. We mostly played covers but a few originals I wrote snuck their way into the song lists. *Love Belongs* is one such song and it gave Just Jake a chance to jam. The lyrics are simple but there is a large complicated vocal finish to this song that was aided by the voice of Sally Walker. Sally appears on many of my albums, performing harmonies, and was the lead vocalist to Just Jake. Her forte is jazz vocals so she can hang in a crowded vocal presence as well as anyone I have ever sung with.

Love Belongs

Love belongs to those who can let go
Love belongs to the heart and to the soul
Love belongs to those who let it grow
Love belongs to those who let it go

Love in circles all around is waiting to be found

At some point, Zephyr began to host a weekly Sunday evening potluck and sauna at our house. We had a pond built in 1985 and then we constructed a sauna house right beside the pond. Prior to the sauna being available, we had constructed many sweat lodges and shared the Native American ritual of sweating together from water poured on rocks heated outside the lodge and then brought inside. The intention was always to cleanse both physically, mentally, and spiritually. We would share prayers, songs, and chants as we sweated together. Several times Native American elders visited Floyd and led ceremonies for those who gathered. We were also blessed over the years by the presence of Chris Deerheart, a friend who always led a beautiful, meaningful lodge. We were fortunate to have those connections. The Native way of life can no longer express itself the way it did centuries ago. However, their reverence for the earth and all of life is still carried forward in rituals that are timeless. I often reflect on the need for a restoration of this reverence as we plunge forward in our culture based on me-first consumerism.

One of many circle gatherings, circa 1989

One ritual from Native traditions that we adapted for our community is the use of a talking stick. Whenever we meet, we try to allow the person who is speaking to have total attention. This is symbolized by the person speaking holding the talking stick which we created from a literal stick with other objects of interest to us attached to it. We occasionally have meetings to discuss a wide variety of issues that can arise when living together and managing a parcel of land. The talking stick makes visible a kind of respect to the process of sharing that deepens our ability to trust each other regardless of the issues at hand.

Zephyr also hosted equinox and solstice gatherings on our farm. The fall equinox was a particularly large event here for many years drawing between 75-100 people annually. Those celebrations arose out of pagan traditions, and we shared songs, invocations and prayers acknowledging the cyclical nature of our time here on Mother Earth. There was always a huge potluck with folks sharing much of the bounty of many gardens grown by those in attendance. We still occasionally engage in a winter solstice ceremony in Jayn's backyard.

The commitment to Blue Mountain School ultimately led to the purchase of land and the construction of a school building. With grades preschool through seven there was a need for a sizable building. Under the architectural direction of Chris Prokosch (the bass player on several of my early recordings and in the band Just Jake) and with much volunteer labor the building came into being. This also provided a community space for gatherings of all sorts. I invited anyone interested in spontaneous song or chanting to come together every other week in the evening at Blue Mountain School. A singing group called the Celebration Singers arose out of these sessions and we performed many times at local festivals and gatherings.

I also developed a workshop called Rise Up Singing that I shared at Unity Churches in later years. Throughout all these experiences, many chants and circle songs came through me in an immediate spontaneous manner. At times, it seemed like all I had to do was reach into the present energy and a song would arrive. Many disappeared into the moment, but several ended up being part of my or the groups I sang with repertoire.

My third album, released on cassette, was entirely based on these chants and circle songs. It was released in 1990 and titled *Light in the*

Wind, a chant that came to me during a sauna. Here are the lyrics to all the chants and songs released on *Light in the Wind*. Several were later released on CD format and are online but most never made it off the cassette.

*The titles that have an asterisk after them are available for listening online.

Light in the Wind *

I am the light in the wind
I am the sound in the beginning
I am the space in between
You know what I mean, forgiveness
I am the light in the wind
I am the sound in the beginning
I am the space in between
I am what I need, forgive me.

Step Lightly on the Earth

Gonna step lightly on the earth, gonna move where the spirit's climbing
Gonna step lightly on the earth, gonna bend and sway with the timing.

This is the Place

This is the place where the power descends
Let the songs begin and our hearts will mend

4 Winds

Let the 4 winds take us, take us along
Let the 4 winds take us, take us home
    Wabun. Shawnodese, Mudjekeewis, Waboose

Wheels Turn

Wheels turn, wheels turn
Any friction we create will burn, burn, burn
Wheels turn, wheels turn
We create our reality to learn, learn, learn

45

My Only Purpose
(from A Course in Miracles)

My only purpose is the one God gave me

Welcome the Way *

Welcome the way we grow
Welcome the way we grow
Open and we will know
Open and it is so.

I Will Not Try

I will not try to love you,
 I will find a place that is in my heart for you
I will not try to know you
 I will find a place that is in my life for you
I will not try to trust you
 I will find a place that is in my soul for you
I will not try to change you
 I will find a place that is clear in me for you

Give Up My Defenses

Give Up my defenses, give up all my lies
Welcome the moment, open up my eyes
Walk with the sunshine full upon my face
Give up my defenses, receive loving grace

Walk, Walk, Walk

Walk, walk, walk, the fine line
Talk, talk, talk the design
Wake, wake, wake the dream up living here forever (together)

Bring Peace to the World *

Bring Peace to the world
Bring love to your heart
Bring joy to this day of life

Gifts

The wind stirs up, the wind lays low
It penetrates my soul
The sun shines high, the sun shines low
It feeds us with its glow
While the waters flowing on the earth embrace her just to show
How the many gifts that we receive will nourish what we grow.

We Can Shine

We can shine, we can shine,
Let it flow, let it flow, let it flow through your soul
We can shine

Laughter and Tears *

The laughter and tears are part of me
The laughter and tears will set me free
I will laugh and I will cry until the day I die
Then I'll leave all the laughing and I'll leave all the crying up to you.

Dance in the Light

Dance in the Light, Dance in the light
Dance, dance, dance, dance, dance
Dance in the light

I Am Sustained by the Love of God

This life gives me everything that I ask it for
It's more than my mind can see
If I'm only looking through these two eyes
I'm missing what really lifts me
    I am sustained by the love of God
Now I wouldn't doubt there are times when I'm down
The laughter can't even reach me
But what I'm forgetting in my ego's pride
Is the only one hurting is me
    I am sustained by the love of God

The pleasures of living are fine that's for sure
And enough is enough til I want more
Being contented with singing this song
Is all that I'm really here for
    I am sustained by the love of God

From beginning to end I am here for today
My changes won't stop, no way
Through sickness and sorrow, hard work and good play
I'm lifted by love everyday
    I am sustained by the love of God

You've Given Me *

You've given me the walk that can take me far
You've given me the talk that I share
And the love of the earth is what I can rebirth everywhere

You've given the light shining in my heart
You've given me the will to be here
Through the calm and the storm my peace will be reborn everywhere

You've given my eyes to see so clear
You've given me memories to return
And the love of all kinds is what will heal and bind and repair

You've given me the silence to know myself
You've given the moments of prayer
And when I hear your voice, I'm given a new choice to be clear

You given me the laughter that fills my heart
You've given me the warmth of the sun
In my dreams I roam far and play amongst the stars with everyone.

You Know Hu

You know Hu we are
You know Hu we are
You know Hu, you know Hu
You now Hu we are

    These chants and songs led me directly to discovering Unity churches. I was visiting a musician friend Laura Light in Charlottesville, Virginia, one weekend and she suggested that I accompany her to the Unity she attended. She shared that she knew the music director and that I would be able to lead some chants during the service. What followed opened my heart and blew my mind in a very positive way. The service was fun and I did get to lead songs that were well received and fully participated in. I had cassettes with me that sold like hotcakes after the service. The whole experience opened another world of opportunity and brought me to people who shared my vision and pursued life in a manner I could respect. My relationship with Unity brought many wonderful people into my life that I never would have known otherwise.

GARDEN IN BLOOM

Involvement with Blue Mountain School ultimately led me to meet Frank Greenlee who recorded my first two cassettes and my first CD. As a fundraiser for Blue Mountain School, I got the idea of creating a recording with some contributions from others and myself material wise. Elizabeth McCommon, a woman singer songwriter friend, suggested Frank. We arranged a time to record about 30 people who gathered in a large barn to sing some familiar chants and circle songs. I was responsible for about half the material we sang as well as the title track. The recording was called Celebration Space. It went well and I realized I could record with Frank in his studio. Our relationship turned into a wonderful collaboration.

Sometime in the fall of 1986, I moved my acoustic piano into Frank's studio that was over an hour's drive away. It seemed like a huge endeavor, but I wanted the piano sound to be genuine and this seemed the best way to accomplish that. I had it tuned, and we used it for my first recording, Treasures in the Stream. It was an adventure bringing people with me to Frank's place and I have always felt much gratitude for the many miles traveled and time contributed by so many to the creation of this music. The songs *The Choice-Rise Up Singing* and *Freedom Eyes* involved the Celebration Singers. At least ten folks showed up and I had the choir I needed for those songs to really kick.

Frank was also a very good guitarist, and I asked him to take a crack at the lead on *The Choice-Rise Up Singing*. When I heard what he did I was amazed! He lifted the song to another dimension. After around 25 trips to the studio, we had a completed project. The songs *The Treasure, Rise Up Singing, We Live Inside a Body, A Child Was Born, Freedom Eyes* and *I Love You Friend*, along with an instrumental, *Daddy Long Legs*, made up this album. There were two additional songs, *Star Eyes* and *One Part (You Don't Gotta be Wild)*, that were part of the cassette but never released on CD.

To release this cassette and any of my future recordings I needed artwork for the covers. I am blessed to have many artist friends who contributed their fine work to my cassette or CD jackets. These folks included William Cox, Isa Graefe, Victoria Stone, Lee Stone, my daughter, Amy, and John Sledd. If you wish to further explore their artwork, several have websites that I list under the heading of Creative Friends at the end of this book. I also used several photographs that I took over the years.

My second album release was *Circles Returning*. To begin this recording, I decided to walk from Zephyr to Travianna, another intentional community in Floyd. I felt the need to let go of everything as I entered the studio. This 12-mile walk was a ritual way of accomplishing that. Travianna is where A'Court Bason lived, an artistic talented musician who had a studio where I would record some of this cassette. A'Court played a multitude of international percussive instruments, many of which he made. He contributed interesting percussive tracks to many songs I recorded with him. I had brought a tent and food over the day before my walk. I stayed there three nights sleeping in the tent. The second night I caught another dream song that became the title track to this recording, Circles Returning. A'Court was a night owl and slept in that morning. It was noon before I got to hit the record button and I am certain I entertained some anxious moments wondering if what I heard in my head was going to work out. By the end of the afternoon the song was tracked. It ended up being the title track for the cassette. The song has a rhythm feel that invokes Native American dance.

Circles Returning

There are prophecies about to come true
There are circles returning into view
There are people who will have to take a stand
For the power to return to the land
    What will we do? It's up to me and you.

There are messages that turn us to the light
If we're bold enough, we never have to fight
For each of us deserves to live in peace
It's the fools we've been that brings us to our knees.
    What will we do? It's up to me and you.

*I keep dreaming of a place where freedom is divine
Where what I know and what I feel at partners in my mind
Where children have a future that's truly theirs to be
And each of us was everything that we were meant to be
    Shine on, shine on, shine on*

*The women are waking in rebirth
Their being can teach us all our worth
The men must learn a gentle heart and hand
What we've done must change, do you understand?
    What will we do? It's up to me and you.*

*Reclaim the joy in our lives
The sparkle can return to our eyes
And all of us can see who we are
A light so bright it shines like a star
    What will we do? It's up to me and you*

*I keep dreaming of a place where freedom is divine
Where what I know and what I feel at partners in my mind
Where children have a future that's truly theirs to be
And each of us was everything that we were meant to be
    Shine on, shine on, shine on*

For this recording the basic tracks were done with A'Court. The drums and some additional vocal work with Frank. There is some outstanding saxophone provided by Billy Bell and backup vocals on both cassettes by Sally Walker and the Celebration Singers.

The songs *Love Belongs* and *Jumping Up and Down Together* are on this album. There were two instrumentals titled *Waterfall* and *Camel's Hump*, both of which were later released on the album *Rewind*. I was always interested in putting an instrumental song on all of my vocal recordings and managed to eventually accomplish this on most of my recordings. The final songs on this cassette were *The Fool* and *Dance in the River*, neither of which made it to the CD.

Circles Returning was released in early 1989 and provided the means to record *Light in the Wind* next with A'Court and members of the Celebration Singers. At that point I returned to work with Frank. We began recording my first album to be released on CD, *Lifetimes and Ages* on January 15, 1991. Desert Storm was just starting, and my pacifist leanings were aroused. The song *Warriors of the World* was to be a part of this album and I was very enthusiastic about working with Frank again. By now I had electric keyboards, and he did as well, so it was not necessary to transport my piano again.

Early on during this process Frank and I discovered we shared the same birthday only three years apart. We had bonded strongly, and this only added to the warmth we shared. Frank died three years ago. I miss checking in with him every now and then. In looking up his obituary I discovered his middle name was Nile. He lived in Egypt the first 12 years of his life. What a cool middle name! Perhaps his energy is aiding in this composition right now as I recall our shared efforts.

The first song on *Light in the Wind* is titled *Awakening / This Journey*. I had recorded the song *This Journey* early on in our process but left about two minutes in front of the tracks to create the intro. This introduction space became a flourishing instrumental, *Awakening*. It ended up being the last thing we did on the recording. It worked beautifully. The album starts with a birthing song and ends with a leaving song with songs of life in between.

Awakening / This Journey

On this journey within I take one breathe to begin it
There are visions from the past and the future leaps up so very fast
    So I give it all away, heal myself today
    Give it all away feel my heart today
Honesty begins when I really listen
Open hand and heart will reappear in a flash of light
    So I give it all away, heal myself today
    Give it all away feel my heart today
When loneliness sweeps in, I remember who is thinking
And as I make my life, I remember what I'm given
    So I give it all away, heal myself today
    Give it all away feel my heart today

I did not acquire any electronic equipment until around 1985, but did have an old pump organ and an acoustic piano. I don't recall the exact timing of several songs written during those first years at Zephyr. The title track to *Lifetimes and Ages,* my fourth recorded album, was written while playing the pump organ I had acquired. The lyrics express a sense of expansion beyond the physical experience that I felt in being alive. It also reflected the possibility of past or future lives.

Lifetimes and Ages

There are lifetimes, there are ages while the sun shines the wind blows on
There are beings filled with wonder who are watching as the tide rolls on
When will we wake up and find ourselves laughing

There are children who are waiting, who are wanting to be loved
There are people who are ancient who are hungry to find love again
What if we touched them, would we remember

Laughing, Crying, Holding, Dying
  Can you share the cosmic joke?
  Walk the razor's edge of grief and hope
  Give yourself the chance to heal
  Can you embrace the life you live?
  With every breath you take you give
  And always let go.

There are colors in the morning, there are shadows in the sun
There is freedom, sweet freedom, if we listen the songs keep being sung
Sing to discover and you'll remember

There are lifetimes, there are ages while the sun shines the wind blows on

During the late 1980s, songs began to appear to me in many different ways. One night, I was nailed by a song in my dreams that was so vivid I woke up with the first and second verses and the refrain already done. It took another 45 minutes for two more verses to form. In the dream I was singing the song with a group of black women who had their hair all done up in tall buns over their heads. The song has a clear antiwar message that resonated with my spiritual and peace-making beliefs. It was performed for many decades after (very often with Grace Note) and occasionally I still pull it out. This song appears on two CDs, *Lifetimes and Ages* and *Red Ripe Apples*. The second version is a live recording done in a studio.

Warriors of the World

Hey there's so many of you, you think you're being cool
Well I got news for ya, your just being fools
There was a time for fighting, that time has come and gone
Now's the time for righting all the hurts and wrongs

Refrain:
>*Warriors, warriors of the world,*
>*Give up your ways, give up your ways*
>*Warriors, warriors of the world*
>*You cannot change what you've done*
>*You cannot carry the gun, without pain without pain*

The little children know, if they're gonna get to grow
You've got to make a change, your games must rearrange
Why can't you talk it out, hey it's ok to shout
Your bombs they won't protect you, if they fall, they won't neglect you
Refrain:

Your thinking is bizarre, paranoia drives you far
Into the dark insane where you play your games
This planet knows your scars, the pain is yours mine it's ours
We are all free to feel so cut to what's real
Refrain:

So many ways to kill, you made it a practical skill
You rule by fist and fear, but a change is here
You know we're gonna live in a world that can forgive
When peace returns to all you will join the call
Refrain:

Warriors, warriors of the world
Give up your ways, give up your ways
Warriors, warriors of the world
The light is breaking thru
It reaches me and you, without pain, without pain

One of my favorite songwriters over the years has been Leonard Cohen. I wrote my own *Hallelujah Song* in response to his famous track. In

Hallelujah Song I engaged members of the Celebration Singers for a big vocal finish. They also contributed to the song *Lifetimes and Ages*. My way of working with vocalists in the studio was to sing their parts to them as they came to me while we were recording. I could hear them in my head and just trusted they would arrive and arrive they always did.

Hallelujah Song

Maybe this song will sound familiar to you
Someone wrote it out long ago
But I gotta sing the words that they cannot say, before they drift away.
Refrain:
> *Ah you never can sing hallelujah enough times*
> *You only will know the way you go when you're gone*
> *Just maybe you'll find enough love in your song*
> *So sing it out clear for those who are here to carry on*

Have you ever cried out in the darkness of night
Just to let the spirits guide you on
So many people hang onto their fright, if they'd let it drift away
Refrain:

Maybe this time will feel familiar to you
We prepared the way long ago
Through the fields of thought to the face of this world
We will rise to clear the way
Refrain:

Hallelujah, hallelujah hallelujah!!!!!!

Up until this point I had shied away from writing many songs about relationships. One slipped through on *Lifetimes and Ages*. It was about my struggles with Jayn and our relationship at the time. My confusion is evident in this song. Digging into this part of my life would take years to resolve. I sensed all of this would provide me with the opportunity for the deeper understandings I was in need of.

Keep My Heart Open

You say that you love me, and I know it's true
And all that's required is to be desired and keep my heart open to you
I know that we're different from the things that we choose
And when we're together I want to remember that I can be touching you
Still I hem and I haw come close and then fall on my knees
Become ice and then thaw, no wonder you tire of me
You say you want safety, release from this fear
I don't want to hurt you or ever desert you, then something else always appears
And when we get closer sometimes I shut down
When my wings should protect you, embrace and respect you
I fly away like a clown

Refrain:
    Still in darkness and light everything is alright
    In heaven I asked for a sign
    Then this song came along, it ain't right it ain't wrong
    If I'm open, I know our love will go on.

You ask me this question, do you want to break thru
I give you this answer, I want to surrender
Stop breaking my heart in two
If there is but one love forgiven and true
I know it surrounds me, lifts up and astounds me
Be open so it will shine thru
Refrain:

You say that you love me, and I know it's true
And all that's required is to be desired and keep my heart open to you

A theme in several songs I have written involved our relationship with the earth. *Calling Calling* is perhaps the best example of that pursuit. I have not played this song out much, but I have listened to it as much as any song I have recorded. The complex harmony at the end of the song was achieved with the help of Sally Walker. The lines *"What can we honor of this Spirit that we are of, that we are. What can we cherish of this spirit that we are of, of the earth"* perhaps says a great deal about our disconnect from nature in this time of environmental crisis.

Calling Calling

How soft the rain falls around me,
Calling calling in quiet harmony
It's bringing life to everything I see,
Don't ask for nothing it's absolutely free

The sun comes out ain't raining anymore
Listen to the wind
We take such pleasures from living everyday
This spirit moves within
It's calling to me, calling to you, calling for us to see

How sweet the shores rhythm can appear
Calling calling for those who wish to hear
It's giving life so much for us to share
We cast our nets out the fruit is always there

The sun comes out ain't raining anymore
Listen to your dreams
We take such treasures from living everyday
This spirit moves within
It's calling to you, calling to me, calling for us to see

What can we honor of this Spirit that we are of that we are
What can we cherish of this Spirit that we are of, of the earth.

There is one instrumental song on *Lifetimes and Ages* titled *Redeemer's Gate*. It was rather experimental for Frank and me, as we used a very early computer-generated drum machine that Frank had built. The song features a piano lead line with drums pushing the song and strings smoothing it out. There is a passage near the end of the song where the music shifts and I always visualized a gate opening which led to the title of the song.

The last song on this album is a song written to honor the passing of many people in my life and specifically my grandfather, S. Guy Johnson. This wrapped up the theme of *Lifetimes and Ages*—from birth to death—very appropriately.

Go Lightly

Walk your path living straight with all
Lift your eyes as your feet move lightly
Measure not how far you fall
Like the river who feeds the ocean

When the sparrow holds you again
When the night wind whispers your name

Listen with your heart be still
All your questions will soon be answered
Measure not how much you know
Trust each breath to provide completely

When the dolphins hold you again
When the night wind whispers your name
Go lightly oh go lightly, go lightly oh go lightly walk in stars

When our mother holds you again
When her heartbeat calls out your name
Go lightly etc.

As the seasons chant you their song
Be your part as if you were dancing
Measure not how long you live
Give each moment your full attention

When our laughter holds you again
When our teardrops whisper your name
Go lightly etc.

I was fortunate to be able to have my early recordings played on the local Public Radio station in Roanoke. At that time, one of the evening shows was put together by Jeff Hunt who promoted local music. Jeff would interview me as each song was played. We really enjoyed each other's company and became good friends. The evening after *Lifetimes and Ages* was played, I jumped into my trusty old Datsun and headed home. I didn't get very far. As I was turning a corner in Roanoke the car just quit running. I managed to get off the road and proceeded to find a phone booth to call my mechanic, Gene Gillespie. Mind you, it was after midnight, and I was hesitant to bother him but alas I didn't know what else to do. His wife answered the phone and told me he was on his way home from his job in Roanoke and would call me at the phone booth when he got in. It is an hour drive but soon he responded. Gene hooked up his trailer and returned to Roanoke. By 4am we were back in Floyd, and he dropped me off at my home! Gene was my mechanic and friend until his death 10 years ago. I was blessed to know this kindhearted man!

Grace Note is Born

Throughout the 1980's music slowly became a bigger part of my life and song writing was a key aspect of that development. The county housed many musicians, and I was privileged to play at gatherings, parties and occasionally at gigs with many of them. One individual who gradually became a bigger part of my life was Tom Williams. Tom and I shared similar families with each of us having two daughters. I actually attended the birth of his first daughter, Cara, at his homestead in another area of Floyd County. We also shared a somewhat similar perspective on the spiritual and cultural evolution of our times. Tom played a nylon stringed acoustic guitar, and we started occasionally putting songs together that I had written along with a few chosen covers. We didn't play many gigs as a duo, but we continued to evolve as musicians. Martin Scudder joined us in early 1990 and this changed everything.

Martin and his dad were building a house at Zephyr for the Giesslers. One day at the end of his workday I wandered up to the site and met Martin and began discussing music with him. I found out he played the violin and I invited him to come play with Tom and I just to see what we might create. A few days later we gathered in my small music studio on the farm and almost immediately the magic started happening. Our voices blended easily. And all of us were quick to find harmony places. The combination of acoustic guitar, violin (which soon became electric violin) and keyboards was unique. And so, it began.

For the next 15 years we made music together and released two albums together that reflected the sound we had created and our musical development. This first album recorded with Grace Note was *I Always Dreamed of Flying*, released in 1993. The recording took place in the studio of Jay Fattorossi or Jay Bones as he was called then (He now goes by Jaris). We did several of the songs live and this gave some added energy that was welcome as we never added drums or bass since we rarely performed with these instruments live. We wanted people to take home what they witnessed live. There are times I wish we had added those instruments as some folks expect to hear drums and bass when listening. This is particularly true online where streaming is now the means of most accessibility.

Tom Williams, me, and Martin Scudder circa 1992

The title song came out of a series of flying dreams that I discussed with Tom. We both were having these experiences in our dreams and so I decided to write about it. The song became one of our favorites to play and also yielded a long jam with us each taking leads. As the years have passed, I have come to enjoy playing this song as much as any I have ever written. It is familiar in a way that led me to the title of this book. There is a lot of room for innovation and the lyrics have become more relevant each day. My heart still wants to witness a world built on loving and not despair. I have come to believe that it is up to me to express this manner of living if I wish to experience this in the world around me.

I Always Dreamed of Flying

I always dreamed of flying, then I left the ground
And I found myself up so high and I 'm looking at the stars all around
I really was suspended, waiting to come down
When I opened up both my eyes this is what I actually found
 Little children all alone
Big people they got no homes
Mother earth on the run
Crazy people got all these guns

Still always have this faith that it will work out
Like a carpenter at the lathe, I keep turning what is inside out
The situation is changing, like a bold sunset
This multicolored mystery here's a vision of what we could get

Golden trust to reemerge
As something deeper than the spoken word
Tolerance for every kind
Shifting poles helps us walk a new line

I Always dreamed of Flying won't you join me there
In a world for everyone built on loving and not despair
Built on loving and not despair

A rather ambitious song we recorded was titled *The One, the Dream, the Dance*. This song was based on relating (perhaps idealistically) the Native American way of life prior to the white man's invasion. I also have experienced past life recall of living a native lifestyle that fed into the creating of this song. We always got a very strong positive response when we performed this song. At the time I had acquired an O1W Korg keyboard that allowed me to create some rather lush string sounds as well as add some percussion to our performance. It is always a pleasure to play this song!

The One, The Dream, The Dance

Long ago in the forest with the wild things we were born
Raised together brother sister drank the water from the horn
Full of plenty from our mother, Earth was in us, we in her
All the stories made us stronger, as the sweat poured from our soul
    And we woke up as the day broke

Quiet hearts full of thanks
Raising songs to the Maker
Of the One the Dream the Dance

And wind calls out to eagle, as wolf howls in the dark
Mother otter, brother bull elk walk in river and mountain shelf
All the world forms of this journey, moss leave stone wood and smoke
Are the powers we respected, we are home within our part
   And we woke up as the day broke
   Quiet hearts full of thanks
   Raising songs to the Maker
   Of the One the Dream the Dance

Now this memory is like a sweet scent we have breathed in then forgot
Our connection to each other all of life's blood cannot be bought
All of life's blood cannot be bought
   Will we wake up stop the hurting
   Heal our hearts be full of thanks
   Raising songs to the Maker
   Of the One the Dream the Dance

Another dream song appeared during this time. I was dreaming with the song *Freedom Eyes* happening, when suddenly it morphed into a different song all together. With a very similar title but a very different feel, the song *Freedom Rise* appeared. Grace Note often played these two songs back-to-back in concert. I started this song with the refrain as it allowed people to learn it quickly and sing along throughout the song.

Freedom Rise

Refrain: Freedom rise like a sunrise 3x oh freedom rise

In this life that we're living
There is pain and strife there is joy and giving
There is searching for truth and delivering
Planting seeds of peace every day
Refrain:

We are here for just one moment
Like a shooting star we may burn and die

And the Trail we leave is the love we've seen
Like the tracks of tears from our eyes
Refrain:
And if freedom don't come your way
You've got to stand up put your shackles away
You've got to lift your heart to the morning sun
That shines so bright for everyone.

It's a simple song that's worth singing
Though it don't take long it's the act of bringing
All the voices gathered together
Won't you join me and sing along
Refrain:

A constant challenge in being alive is change. Some part of me often wants to be with what is familiar and resists the many changes that often occur seemingly beyond my control. I suspect this is true of all of us. Adapting or allowing change certainly makes the path forward easier. The song *Crossroads* was my attempt to put a perspective on this quandary.

Crossroads

Entering the crossroads,
Looking for a sign to point my way, you know what I feel
Stand in contemplation
Thoughts inside my mind from where the ebb and flow are the same
  Refrain:
    One road makes me stronger, one road has no end
    Each path has distinction, each one is my friend.

Softly go my footsteps
I could just as well have fallen down or chosen to remain
No more hesitation
Breath into my heart and make my way I'm safe once again
Refrain:
    One road makes me stronger, one road has no end
    Each path has distinction, each one is my friend.

Now I see beside me
Pilgrims on a path to peace to find a way to live as one
Weaving sacred footsteps

A tapestry of life beyond the dance that we've begun
Refrain:
> *One road makes me stronger, one road has no end*
> *Each path has distinction, each one is my friend.*

One of my close friends at this junction in life was a woman, Isa Graefe. We shared an evening of dance together that inspired the song *Riding the Design*. Dancing has always been an inspiring experience for me. I attended many events called Dance Free in Boston and have continued to get up and dance whenever the opportunity presents itself. It just makes me smile! There are two released versions of this song. The first is with Grace Note on this album and 20 years later I did a full band version on *Stay Above the Radar*.

Riding the Design

We could have danced all night and you know it
We could have sung to the mountains and the moon
We took a chance on the dance and you know it
Helped the love come thru for me and you

Oh the light in your eyes was a showing
And that light told me what we feel
We took a chance on that light and the glowing
Helped the love be real for me and you.

Every single day people want to say I love
Stupid little fears creep into our ears instead
Walking a fine line riding the design inside you
It's easy when you trust, trust the one you're with

And the stories we told we're quite ancient
They were built in the castles and the runes
And I remember the gifts and the knowing
Helped the love come thru for me and you Refrain:

Now there are old ways that come from the jungle
And drums are still beating like the rain
For the heart of rhythm is among us
When the love comes thru for me and you

Both Grace Note albums concluded with songs that I wrote at the very end of the recording process. The song *For Everyone* showed up while we were recording. Martin and Tom were kind enough to work it out and add it as a wrap up song. I ended several albums with songs that had an appeal for us all to find our higher nature while living on this earth. This is one such song.

For Everyone

I have walked many roads
Sometimes all alone
And this world still seems a place to me, to be
For everyone whose laughter only echoes in a hurting heart
For everyone whose hunger is insane
For everyone whose liberty and freedom are still denied
For everyone who stood to take the blame
    In a world with so much pain
    It is time for us to change, and seasons change
For everyone who loves the clouds as much as they love the sun
For everyone whose climbed a mountain trail
For everyone who loves the feel of sand between their toes
For everyone whose stood still in the rain
    In this moment I recall there is room enough for all
    Raised on reason our faith is short on time
    It is treason to separate with lines one world, one world
For everyone to find to find a love that fits inside their heart
For everyone to grow beyond their dreams
For everyone to see just how they fit into their part
For everyone to find out what it means
For everyone to find a love that fits inside their heart
For everyone to grow beyond their dreams
    In this moment I recall there is room enough for all
    Room for all, room for all

Three songs from my earlier recordings were part of the Grace Note repertoire. *Freedom Eyes, Live Inside A Body* (a live version) and *Strong Foundation* all made it onto this Grace Note CD. There was also a very melodic instrumental titled Nightshades on which Tom played the Native American flute, Martin played violin and I played keyboard. It was tracked live. Tom contributed a song *Timeless Age* and Martin chipped in a fun instrumental *Dragonfly*. This process brought us closer together and gave us more reason to travel for concerts, mostly to Unity churches in the mid-Atlantic area. We were not road warriors as each of us had busy lives apart from the music, but those shared times were fun and we made a lot of friends during those years.

Keep the Light Burning

As my participation in music deepened so did the frequency of songs appearing. As a result, I had enough new songs to tackle another solo album, produced in the mid-nineties. This recording, *Keep the Light Burning*, was manifested in Jay Bones' studio again. The process was spread out over a couple of years and included both inspiring and frustrating moments. It was the first time I invited musicians who just didn't perform as I had hoped they would and that left me searching for either a different way to complete songs or letting them go. All of this eventually enriched the project and helped me broaden my skills as an arranger and producer in the studio.

The first song on the album, *Who Knows What Will Come*, puts into play several basic questions about living here, in these times. The idea that we can control our future has permeated into our western culture. From New Age thinking that we are responsible for everything we experience, to the idea that our thoughts create our reality (they may be an assist IMHO) to ideas that how long we live is in our control, to the idea of karma there is much that we just don't seem to want to admit arrives unannounced and out of our control. Yet this gives all of us the opportunity to practice radical acceptance in our daily affairs and perhaps find creative ways to express our gratitude for the very gift of life we have been given. These themes run throughout *Keep the Light Burning*.

Who Knows What Will Come

When all the questions of these days
Get so overwhelming that you say
Couldn't we find another way?
Free from all this worry and waste
Who knows what will come?

And when you feel your teardrops burn
What's bringing on this sadness, can we learn?
How to be sharing the gifts of this world
Stop with all this madness turn, turn, turn
It's bringing on this sadness, can we learn?

How to hear the sound that's searching in the wind
To remind you that your life was freely given
    And there are millions and billions of souls
    Searching for wisdom, just wanting to grow
    Who knows what will come?

And as we travel life' highways
Looking for love and friendship everywhere
Our disappointments seem to say
How can we get together?
How can we get together through it all?

Can we hear the sound that's searching through the wind
To remind us that our lives are freely given
    And there are millions and billions of souls
    And there is wisdom just wanting to grow
    Yes there are millions and billions of souls
    Living in nature and wanting to grow
    Who knows what will come?

Steppin' Into Heaven is a song that Grace Note performed at Unity churches for many years. The lyrics focus on how to be present in this Here and Now.

Steppin' Into Heaven

Steppin into heaven on earth to be all that we are
Living with a notion, an instinct for change
Burning all the bridges, the pictures of what we once were
Turning all the suffering and hatred to gain
    Oh so many wise, open your eyes
    Call out and they will come thru
   Listen to the wisdom with patience and look past the veil

Complement each other and give what you got
Holding onto to nothing and dancing to the beat of your heart
Telling all the stories and sharing your part
    So many wise open your eyes
    Call out and this will come true

The third song on this album asks the question; what is the pulse of life? The form of the song took a nice surprise when it morphed into a kind of call-and-return in a round as the question was asked. You may guess the answer I came up with. Read on through the lyrics and see if you agree!

The Pulse of Life

What is the pulse of life?
What are the lessons learned?
Is it a cry for peace? Is it the desert burned?

What is the pulse of life?
Is it the season's turn?
Is it the morning sun? Is it the full moons' burn?
Everyone looks for the answers
To questions that run through our minds
God's grace could be given if asked for
When we look with our hearts and we will find
    Love is give and forgive
What is the pulse of life?
Why are we born alone?
Is it the bird in flight? Is it the vultures' bone?

What is the pulse of life?
What are these words we share?
Is it the lovers' wish? Is it the rays of prayer?
How precious this time we recover
The will and the way to be free
To lift ourselves up with each other
To honor, to trust and to see
    Love is give and forgive

What is the pulse of life? Love Is

Love, whether that is universal or personal, seems to inspire songwriters, and I am no exception. The following three songs were inspired by relationships I entered in the mid-late 90's after my divorce from Jayn in 1994. There will be more about this theme in my life later. *I Want to Thank You* was written as a thank you note to a new love in my life. After the release of the album, I realized I had allowed this song to go on too long, something I would wrestle with several times in song production.

I Want to Thank You

Your love has blessed me, given me so much more
Than I can say, than I can show you
And in your heartbeat, I feel the pulse of life
And in my soul, I know this is true

Refrain: I want to thank you yes, I want to thank you
For knocking on my door
Risking all that came before to give yourself to love

And in this moment that we have brought to bear
We've sojourned so far so far from home
And like spring flowers buried so deep below
Quiet and free they wait to grow
Refrain:

> *Every day there's a way, what's inside cannot hide*
> *To forgive is to live*

I want to thank you for being strong and clear
With heart so full of care and give yourself to love
Refrain:

Harmlessly Bountiful

How'd you learn to shine so bright, I feel you miles away
How'd you turn your pain upright, you shape it just like clay
Whispering like a stream, you live free so it seems
Life will bloom wherever it flows

When you shed your tears divine do they touch the earth?
Fall around your feet like wine, sparkling seeds of birth
Balancing what you can trust with me
What you know you can feel, and so much to feel

All the healing that life provides
We learn how to live, how to surrender and how to die

And How'd you heal the wounds won't hide
And when they show themselves
They call like warriors battling til death becomes itself
Oh to be merciful, harmlessly bountiful
One with spirit calling and love

So I see there's no alternative but to be yourself
All of life compels us forward work becomes itself
Oh to be merciful, harmlessly bountiful
One with Spirit calling and love

The Key

Turn the key look at me I'm still standing here
All alone almost home you whisper in my ear
Call my name touch the flame burning in my heart
Feed the fire of desire and faith when we're apart

All of life can be cherished here answered as a prayer
Every night we let go of fear calling, calling my dear

It's a dream so it seems living life as art
Living free conceived to be calling, calling, calling my dear

The following song, *Tears Will Roll Away,* was another dream song, and it contains a lyric that amazed me when it came through. The song is a cappella and became a favorite to share when I was singing at Unity churches. The lyrics to this song appeared to me to be full of instruction on how to be here in this world. As is often the case, the song wrote itself to give me a bit of guidance that I still am learning to apply.

Tears Will Roll Away

If you're living life within the laws
Of paradise effect and cause
Will give to you just what you take
So love yourself for heaven's sake
    And your tears will roll away so sweetly

When the seasons move too quick for you
And the tender years are out of view
Make a miracle out of every step
It'll bring you home with no regrets
    And your years will roll away so sweetly

There's someone who can give to you
A measure of respect you're due
A patient ear when you're in need
A gentle push when you must bleed
    And your tears will roll away so sweetly

    Time is never on your side
    Its' presence is a test
    For those you love will challenge you
    To give your life and all you love
    This moments' very best

The gift for you in being here
Is to recognize your deepest fears
To heal the wounds you self-inflict
So the words you speak won't contradict
    And your tears will roll away so sweetly

The light inside you'll probably find
Will take you out of your confines
For all of life is waiting there
The star fields are the clothes you'll wear
    And your tears will roll away so sweetly

The first time I performed this song after *Keep the Light Burning*'s release, I had a rather interesting insight. The cover of the CD is a painting done by my friend, amazing artist and human being, Lee Stone. Lee and I had become good friends, often staying together while attending craft fairs. The picture shows a human figure floating in space. The figure is blue and covered with stars. As I sang the last verse "*and the star fields are the clothes you'll wear,*" I just smiled a deep acknowledgement of how tight this universe can be. Lee had not heard the music prior to making the cover and yet here was a visual line from this song. Sometimes making a miracle out of every step is just the way it is!

The last three songs on this album were all of a nature that they arrived like a message. In fact, the title of one is *The Message*. My shaded optimism pushes through the lyrics. It's a gift to see all life's harmony, with humility and kindness. We are currently being tasked to see that harmony.

The Message

From the words of the prophets the time is at hand
If you look all around you, you'll understand
There's a love that is growing but it's not a command
It's a welcoming knowing, not a demand
    All the blessings show it.

See all the colors streaming between us
There is such a rich texture we are learning to trust
Our reasoning's noble it has such a thick hide
But it can't hold a candle to the love inside
    All the children know it

There's a message from the crystal core that rises like a geyser
Like a rainbow blazing full it shows it light to make us wiser
    It's a gift to see all life's harmony

With humility and kindness, you know it!
There's a message from the future child that's rising like a geyser
Please respect the wind and sky, this living skin
And all that comes from Gaia

Pray For Each Other

Pray for each other, keep praying
Sing with each other, keep singing
Dance with each other, keep dancing
Wait for each other, keep waiting

Love is an open, open sea where we can dance in this great mystery
Sailing together in all we can be
Rising to touch every wave
Breathe in the faith to be brave

Play with each other, keep playing
Talk to each other, keep talking
Look at each other, keep looking
Laugh with each other, keep laughing

Laughter is feeling without control
Share it together it's good for the soul
Teardrops can follow and touch what is whole
Heaven is waiting for thee, heaven is wanting to be

Stand in your calm, touch palm to palm and feel
A grateful amen for each rainbow's end we see

Keep the Light Burning

Like the eagles' cry in a dream gone by
There's a vision living still
Or the whippoorwill whose questions thrill
Will the calm return and build
A place where we can breathe in deep and touch in Spirits' will

If the memories return what have we learned
With all this work we've done
Where there's butterfly joy like a newborns' toy
We put fear on the run
Like a blind man on a mountain top staring at the sun
 Refrain:
        Have faith in everyone, the work it will get done

Have faith in everyone, keep the light burning

On a trail in the dark trust is the part
That keeps us moving on
Through the turns and the burns and the seasons' returns
Only change is sure to come
To find that place where we can grow and care for everyone!
Refrain:
  Have faith in everyone, the work it will get done
  Have faith in everyone, keep the light burning

A line from this song struck home soon after this time. *"To find a place where we can grow and care for everyone."* I had an experience around this time where I was the recipient of some fortunate care. I was weeding Jayn's blueberry patch when the hand sickle I used sliced my index finger and thumb on my left hand. I pretty much fileted my finger. It would require 16 stitches. This occurred on a Saturday evening around 7pm. I called a local doctor, Steve Beese, who I knew from attending a Quaker meeting in Floyd. He agreed to meet me in his office around 8pm. After cleaning the wound, he determined I needed a lot of stitches plus I had severed a tendon in my thumb so it would not move horizontally. He called a specialist friend about the tendon. With his advice he sewed the tendon together and we hoped for the best. My hand was immobilized for the next 6 weeks so I did not know if I would be able to play the piano with that thumb in the future. When the apparatus holding my finger and thumb still was removed, my thumb worked as it should. Hallelujah! Also, Steve never charged me for his work but instead told me to pay it forward. Pretty amazing gift that I have tried to repay in spades!

The outro to both *Pray for Each Other* and *Keep the Light Burning* are a climax of the lyrics and energy of the songs. *Pray For Each Other* did not have its final ending until I was returning from playing at Unity in Lynchburg one Sunday and I heard the ending in my head. Upon getting home I immediately went to my piano and worked up what I thought would be the part. I then went to my neighbor, Diane, who sang in the Celebration Singers, and asked her to try this with me, as it was two vocal parts that were very different but sung together. Lo and behold it worked! When I sing this song in churches, I ask the congregations to sing the main body as I sing this new part along with them. Many times, it has given me chills!

What's Dear

The next album in line, *Fragrance of the Rose,* released in 2001, was a return to the studio with Grace Note. At this point Martin had built a nice recording studio, so we began working there. We added a bass player for this project, Gerry Skendarian, who had been playing with us occasionally during this time frame. This album features mostly my songs, again with a lively instrumental by the group (*So You Dance*), as well as two cover songs; *Squirrel Hill* by Jules Shear, and *Somewhere Over the Rainbow* by Arlen and Harburg from The Wizard of Oz. My first online purchase was the rights to use those two songs. It seemed very appropriate at the time and still does! We also did our version of the Shaker hymn, *Gift to be Simple*. Three of the songs were a cappella songs that we frequently performed when in concert.

The title track on this album came into being a week before I played at Unity in Roanoke. The guest speaker that day was a woman who channeled Mother Mary, Ileah Van Hubbard. She invited me to assist her in a workshop she offered that afternoon by adding musical interludes. Ileah used rose petal fragrances in her workshop and spoke several lines that were directly associated with this song. I really had no idea this would happen and the experience of working with her for several months after at other workshops added a great deal of meaning to this song for me. I highly recommend her book Mother Mary's Teachings for the New World. The circumstance of writing the song a week before I met her was another one of life's miracles being manifested.

Fragrance of the Rose

Say hello to the spark that lives within
Growing slow like the flowers in the spring
And you know all the dramas and sideshows
Sacrifice the fragrance of the rose
Steady now, open eyes and open heart
Who could blame you?

You're the brush stroke and the art
And you know when it all falls into place
You can't erase taking chances.
Refrain:
> *It's a pleasure to get on with it*
> *One you may not choose to hide*
> *So just grin and share you luck with heaven knows*
> *It's the fragrance of the rose*

Many days start with shadows from the past
To remind you life's a play and we're the cast
What's your name? Is it honey to the bee?
Spoken easily like an ancient recipe
And your fate, can you close your eyes and see
What will be is surrendered to be free
Touch your heart where the blood flows from the start
And we get the strength for taking chances Refrain:

> *Living all in kindness*
> *Brothers, sisters are we*
> *Living all from the generosity of love's unbroken circle*

So you see life is built on harmony
You and me living in this symphony
And we trust when it all falls into place
We can't erase taking chances
Refrain:

The leadoff song on this album is *Sail*. The song features our three-part harmony, and Martin's violin work amid a lush-feeling arrangement.

Sail

Sail over the mountain, sail to the sea
Sail down the river, sail in the breeze
Open up your eyes to the horizon
In this world you are home

Cry for the losses, cry for songs unsung
Cry with tender mercy, cry from your bones
Open up your heart to the beginning

In this time, you are not alone

Live for each other, live on the edge
Live like a river, live and forgive
Open up your mind to discover
All of life will meet you there

Sail over the mountain rising, rising
Sail to the sea, patiently
Sail down the river, let the waters hold you
Sail in the breeze, spread your wings

Open up your Soul to recover
In this way you are free.
Sail, Sail, Sail

During the recording of this album, I celebrated my 50th birthday on the 28th of February 2000. I invited a host of friends to come to my home and planned a surprise that reflected my deep regard for my friends. I wrote poems for the closest 24 friends and bought small bouquets of flowers for each of them. Those folks arrived early, and I held a kind of ceremony thanking them each for being in my life. In the midst of celebration, however, I learned of the death of a close friend from her partner. I then received a phone call telling me of the death of my Uncle Reg. I had not seen him in years, but I always felt a warm regard for him as he was a jokester and always made my family feel welcome whenever we visited. The party had a somewhat somber feel for me, but the events of the day reminded me how precious it is to be here. I was asked to write a song for my friends' memorial service. The song, *Always There Is Love to Give Away*, made its way onto this *Fragrance of the Rose*. It was written on the guitar which was a first in quite a while.

Always There Is Love to Give Away

As I sit here before me, the empty page is yawning
All my life seems just like a play
There are stormy days then sunshine to make the new day happen
And always there is love to give away

I hear my sister's suffering and I don't know just why
I only ask that what may pass in time
Would be the deep expression of what her soul is yearning
And what our hearts are learning by her side

Refrain:
> Always there is love to give away
> Through the pain and years of tears I give thanks today
> Cause always there is love to give away

I have heard that in forgiving life can be renewed
Hearts restored to be explored again
And though there's nothing certain, there's also nothing lost
Ask and ye shall know that there's a way
Refrain:

So pour the waters over me and cleanse me once again
Hold me like a bird up in the wind
And I will fly beside you forever and a day
There is always love to give away.
Refrain:

Openly Be is a bouncing jazzy tune that Grace Note enjoyed riffing on. I have often wondered if there is such a word as openly, but it sure fits the mode of this songs' lyrics.

Openly Be

Silly singing these suffering songs
When there's so much suffering already going on
I've been thinking about what it would mean
If we all got together and changed this whole scene
Love from your soul can come thru and make us all whole
So you see there ain't nothing that's real
Less you're living like you're willing to take hold of the wheel

Refrain:
> Live your life, live it with ease
> Give yourself every chance to see now
> Live your life openly be
> There's always someone you can give your heart to

Step thru that door, dance on that shore
Give something more and be free

If you're living your life for yourself
Then there won't be room for anyone else
Money, money won't give you no smiles
Just put off your pain for a little while
Empty heart won't find its own cure
Til it finds its own center that is clean and pure
Looking back, I ain't got no regrets
Anything that ain't finished comes around you can bet
Refrain:

One theme of my life that got played out very often in my years as a potter was back pain. The worst of this experience had me crawling for about 6 weeks at one point. Clay and pottery can be heavy. Loading and unloading a kiln involves a lot of reaching forward with weight in your hands, which at the time often was difficult to say the least. I was also cutting around 15 pickup loads of firewood each year for our woodfire kiln, in addition to the firewood necessary to keep us warm. So, to give some levity to the situation I wrote *Bad Back Blues*. This was perhaps Grace Note's favorite song to perform live and always got a big hand. I have recorded it twice. This version has some great harmony in addition to snappy leads by each of us.

Bad Back Blues

Now my backs had lots of uses, but mostly I recall
They are from the fact from head to toe I am over 6 feet tall
When I bend down to the ground I deal with gravity
The consequence of which is sometimes one bad back for me
Just for me to get here I bent down once or twice
And each time I can guarantee I followed this advice
Bend at the knees and keep my back straight
I live by both these rules
And stretch it out when I get home
Cause I don't want to be now damn fool

I got the bad back blues from my head down to my shoes
I got the bad back blues some days it's like a great big bruise

I got the bad back blues I got them bad back blues

When I was just a young lad, so much life in store for me
I thought I'd make the world a better place to be
I figured I'd burn firewood instead of oil you see
The price of gas was going up and wood was almost always free
But little did I realize the cost of that to me
That doggone chainsaw nearly broke my back,
Sometimes it feels like permanently
Now I realize there are things to which I must say no
So don't you even ask me to help you move that old piano.
    I got the bad back blues from my head down to my shoes
    I got the bad back blues if it's heavy I refuse
    I got the bad back blues I got them bad back blues

As years go by, I always try to picture in my heart
A back that's strong and beautiful I mostly fit the part
And when I travel life's highway, I remember it's a long, long road
And I don't have to be the one to carry the heavy load
    I got the bad back blues from my hips down to my shoes
    I got the bad back blues, some days I limp instead of cruise
    I got those bad back blues ah you know I got them blues.

My time at The Brotherhood of Spirit yielded one lifelong friend, Robin Paris. Robin still lived in the main location of the community in a house she had built there. That location is near where my mother's family is from in New Hampshire. I have visited my family there for many decades and often managed to get a visit in with her. We shared a deep trust and interest in things of a spiritual nature that has resulted in a unique friendship that sadly has ended with her death recently. I say ended with a caveat as I know she has moved into a spirit place that reaches beyond the limit of our 50-year friendship. The following song is an a cappella song I wrote with her in mind that I performed almost every concert with Grace Note. I still trot it out for myself once in a while. The lyrics stretch the imagination about what is possibly our true nature and "history".

What's Dear

We were together before the time of rainbows
Before the time of stormy weather
We were a dancing where there was only color
Where there was sound so pure the floor was light beneath our wings
And if we wanted to fly, we just opened our hearts to the sky

Everything was sacred and it really didn't matter
If we were lost or found or high or low
There was such beauty, such everlasting beauty
The only thing that touched our inner eyes
And if we wanted to kiss, we just made a wish and we sighed
    So what happened here
    How did we lose what's dear bye and bye, bye and bye

Living in a body can be so much confusion
Can be so much illusion that we cry
Cry out for mercy, for tender loving mercy
From judgments that we made ourselves in years gone by
And if we want it to change, we accept the pain and realize
    What we're doing here, is loving all those fears
    What we're doing here, is loving all those tears
    And letting them fly, fly, fly

The next song on the album *Fragrance of the Rose* is *Every One of Us Has Got a Name*. The song was written about family and specifically came into being to celebrate the 50th wedding anniversary of my Uncle Steve and Aunt Mary E. He was my mother's oldest brother, and this event was celebrated during our family's reunion in the year 2000 in Winchester, New Hampshire. There were about 45 family members present and together for a week. Family reunions are something my mom's side of the family shared every five years from 1990 until 2015, a year after both my mom and Uncle Steve died.

Every One of Us Has Got a Name

We are born into the family of humankind
Greeted by the heart of love and home
By luck or chance, intent or grace, no one really knows

The blood of ancients runs inside our bones

The names that we all carry are gifts from those who love
To give us birth and care 'til we move on
No task in life is simple and parenting is one
That offers us a love that knows no bounds
Refrain:
> *There are those who stay together fifty years or more*
> *And some who cross the oceans to open up life's door*
> *From sea to sea, we learn to dance on the always changing shore*
> *And every one of us has got a name*

What we make of every moment is only ours to choose
To till the soil, teach or make amends
We labor with a vision of what we came here for
And when we give, we honor what has passed before
Refrain:

Every path is different, no two are the same
And we return from where it is we came
To celebrate our living with laughter song and games
And give thanks for sharing in life's flame
Refrain:

Many of the songs I have written over the years reflect a spiritual overtone. The basics of this were set in play in my youth and expanded as I moved into exploring different religions, different viewpoints within religions, and the relationship of consciousness to our planetary experience. The only Christian churches I have been able to embrace are Unity, Unitarian Universalist and Church of Divine Science. Grace Note performed at Unity churches for decades, as did I solo. I found the people most welcoming and inclusive and their take on the role Jesus played, or plays, more accepting of ideas out of the mainstream. Grace Note also performed seasonally at The Zion Lutheran Church (a progressive church in Floyd) where Martin was a member. They hosted a summer music series at their outside pavilion and Grace Note performed for over a decade there.

Outside of religious institutions, I have found most people are interested in some kind of spiritual exploration, whether it be defined by a tradition or not. Besides Christianity, I also explored Buddhism, Hinduism,

Native American spirituality and beliefs, paganism, and many mediation techniques such as Zen and Vipassana. I did 5 ten-day Vipassana sits under the guidance of S.N. Goenka. Several of these were at a retreat center in Shelburne Falls, Massachusetts, near my New Hampshire relatives, so there was the benefit of visiting before and after. All of this (along with the many books I have read, some I mentioned earlier) has influenced the character of my songwriting. A song that speaks lightly of this is *Something to Believe In* from *Fragrance of the Rose*. This song was written as part of a play that someone asked me to write songs for. It was one of eight songs that were completed for the project, but is the only one that ever made it into a studio for an album. The play never reached a stage unfortunately, but it would have been interesting to work with musicians in that capacity.

Something to Believe In

Sometimes in life we need a real good thing
Doesn't really matter what it is, it's the sweetness it brings
Could be a jelly roll or a snowball fight
Something to believe in with all of your might
   Something to believe in, something to believe
I've learned to be patient with all of my kin
Ain't got much use for criticizing
Some say I'm lonely, some days that's true
Need something to believe in to help me get thru
   Something to believe in, something to believe

I ain't got no excuse
I've done my share of abuse
But I was looking for something to believe in

Everyone's different and I don't mind
Life would be boring if you were my kind
I just can't figure why we carry all this pain
We need something to believe in to lift us up once again
   Something to believe in, something to believe

Two songs appeared on *Fragrance of the Rose* that reflected my idealism in the realm of romantic love, *Great Big Love* and *Love Grow Slow*.

Both songs made use of Grace Note's good vocal harmony to flush out the instrumentation.

Great Big Love

I've been waiting for the love of my life
Waiting for the chance to say hi
And when you got here, I didn't know what it would feel like
Something has opened up wide, can't say that I haven't tried
Everyone knows just what that feels like
Then you stood there right before me
Smiling like I knew you would be
And all I could say was my it's good to see you again
Wouldn't you know you'd be a friend
    Time passes slowly, I like to give
    When you hold me, I like to give
    I open my heart to this great big love

Like a jewel in the desert sand
It's hard to see what we had planned
The fog of the past can make the road look dangerous ahead
Giving up the old, old lies, helps us to open our eyes
To see the signs that guide us on our way
Gotta tell the truth the best that I can
Be open to the boy in the man
And listen to the girl who was scared and finally cried
And then you'll know you've got a friend
    Up on the mountain and out on the sea
    It's an awesome world and we are free
    Wherever you go wherever you are
    There's always this gift that shines like a star up above
    It's this great big love

And when the angels come to stand by my side
All the tears that I have already cried
Will open the door to show me the way home again
When there's nothing left for me to do
But give the touch that says I'll be true
True to the heart that beats in a friend
And after all the loves of my life

Have opened up my heart to its' light
And I'm held in their hands like wine in a fine glass
Wouldn't you know we're friends to the last
    Time passes slowly, I like to give
    When you hold me, I like to give
    I open my heart to this great big love

Love Grow Slow

Oh we've only just met and there's lots of room yet
For me to know your dream
Do you know that I respect you
Wish you all the love you feel
Your smile reaches deep within your silence
It's all that I can do to stop and watch you within mine

And you told me you'd been looking for this opportunity
For someone you could sing with and live in harmony
I laughed and said I knew the feeling
My heart has wondered often how to share this mystery

Refrain:
    How do go slow oh let this love grow slow
    How do I let it go, let it grow and let go
    I reach out, heal my doubt
    Sing this song, carry on

There's so much inside I don't want to hide
Want to feel myself give birth
To the joy I know feel it head to toe
Every breath is full of worth
The sun in all its' morning glory
Returns each day to show us faith and trust in the divine
Refrain:

And I know your life is a sacred song
That you sing with every day
Inspiration in your fingertips like a child discovering clay
The light you welcome every moment

Reveals the ancient memories as we learn again to say
Refrain:

Once again, the last song on *Fragrance of the Rose* was written as we were completing this project. It became a favorite of mine to play at Unity gatherings over the years. The lyrics reach into the challenges of being here and perhaps soothe with the words "*love will leave you whole.*"

Love Will Leave You Whole

When you're crossing the line from life to living
And you don't know just why but you know what you feel
It may be quite hard but you find a way to keep on giving
Cause you know that it's real, it's all part of the deal

> *So open up, open up the fire is gonna shape you*
> *Open up, open up and change it just might break you*
> *But love will leave you whole*

When there's no going back to touch a new tomorrow
And the walls turn to glass, you can't live in the past
If you can't make a mark or a dent in your sorrow
It just takes some time, God knows about time

> *Open up, open up the water's gonna cleanse you*
> *Open up, open up and change it just might break you*
> *But love will leave you whole*

Sun setting sun you're the blessing of the one
Let us not forget the light in shadows

When you're walking a line that looks like circles
Who can explain, go dance in the rain
Don't hold your breath or wait for miracles
It's all right in view, looking for you

> *Open up, open up the fire's gonna shape you*
> *Open up, open up and change it just might break you*
> *Open up, open up the water's gonna cleanse you*
> *Open up, open up earth mother's gonna take you*
> *But love will leave you whole*

Rivers from the Sun

In 1997 I began recording what would become my only fully instrumental album to date, *Rivers from the Sun*. I made heavy use of my Korg O1W for this project. While I had placed instrumentals in all my previous releases and have continued to do so, I had not focused on music of that nature until this point in time. The process of writing this music I can only describe as being "channeled." Most of the 13 songs on the album have a basic track that I reached for and recorded in one take, several times the first time I attempted to play. This was often after a period of emptying myself out, as in meditation, in preparation to reach for the music. Five songs came through me in a few months in 1997 and then it just stopped. I worked in the keyboard's sequencer to embellish those initial tracks but nothing more happened, so I let go of the project for a while.

Then, during a visit in the winter of 2003 with Jill Schneider (my flame at the time) the song *Sunrise on the Shore* came through. She played music as well and I had arranged to have a keyboard shipped to her home in Florida. One morning, I just started playing this piece of music and it stretched on. I had hit record before I started, and I remember as it crossed into over five minutes just holding on for dear life wondering how this would end. It ended beautifully! I was simply full of gratitude.

There was another gap before the music started again, but in the spring and summer of 2004, I received seven instrumentals in the space of several months. I had purchased an 8-track digital recorder and began recording with it. This was much easier to work with than the O1W sequencer, plus I could record other instruments as well. I had two rather modest microphones, which I used in a manner that let me create stereo tracks for the Native American flute, harmonica and recorder that I played on *Rivers from the Sun*.

The first track on the album is titled *Eagle Flies at Dawn*. I asked my friend Chris Deerheart to come play the Native American flute for this piece. I had all the keyboard tracks already completed, but it just didn't work for him. He encouraged me to take a crack at it myself. I possessed a flute in the right key for the song, so I proceeded. After just a few attempts, the track poured through. I named the song *Eagle Flies at Dawn* in honor of a child that Chris and his partner lost in childbirth, and whose body was placed in our graveyard here at Zephyr. This song is by far my most successful, currently receiving between 100 and 150k plays a month on Pandora. The other track that I played the Native American flute on is *Voices in the Wind*. The flute provided not only a melody, but also some interesting, subtle sounds that fit right into the theme of the music.

There are two tracks on *Rivers from the Sun* that feature the piano as a solo lead instrument, *Butterfly* and *Clear Blue*. While recording *Butterfly*, I attempted to visualize a butterfly in flight as it created the notes and phrases I played. The song has a delicate nature that seems to draw listeners in, and it is the second most successful track on the album.

Divinity's Way, *Siren's Song* and *Mediterranean Dream* were all from the 1997 episode of recording. They each have a complexity and spontaneity that arrived with much detailed editing, and trial and error for choice of sounds while working on the O1W.

I played the harmonica on *Ode on A Hill*. I really was uncertain it could work, as the harmonica usually has a shrill character that is not so adaptable to the laid back "new age" feeling I was seeking. What I visualized was a man sitting on a hill playing his harmonica into the open spaces surrounding him and it seemed to work. The result was a lilting, almost echo-filled song.

Waltz of the Lily blends two piano tracks into a play of melody lines that flush out in a rich manner. A somewhat simpler track than others on the album, it was my attempt to share the quiet beauty of the lily.

The title track, *Rivers from the Sun,* was the last song I wrote for the album. I remember the basic track happening quickly, but I did not get a perfect take that I could use. I memorized four minutes of the song and played it over and over until I finally got a "perfect" track. I then played the piano over the top as the "lead" instrument, visualizing the sounds as if streaming from the sun. This song has a power to it that flows from those piano phrases.

The last track on *Rivers from the Sun* is *Homeward Bound*. This song has a Celtic feel, and I played the recorder for the first time in many years. The recorder was an instrument I learned to play in my teen years. I remember playing it with my Aunt Mimi as we tried to perform some duets, myself on soprano and her on the alto. It took me a short while to get my chops back, but this song ended up benefiting from the reemergence of that instrument.

By fall of 2004, I was ready to master all the songs and assemble them into a CD. I did the mastering on that Yamaha 8-track and then took it to my friend, Skip Brown, who ran Awakened Group Studio in Roanoke. Skip had recorded all the vocals for Grace Note on *Fragrance of the Rose* and our connection there led to me working with him for my next three albums. When he did a final master of *Rivers from the Sun,* it took only two hours. I had been lucky enough to get it pretty much aligned with what was desired.

I played everything on this album except for the track *Nightshades* that Grace Note recorded for the *I Always Dreamed of Flying* album. That track fit right in and, in total, the 13 songs came to just under one hour of music. The length proved to be perfect for massage therapists who choose to use this album for their hour-long sessions. *Rivers from the Sun* has a "new age" quality to it, but—as I like to describe it when asked—is not just two chords with fluff layered on top. It has some depth with unexpected movement, and it seems others agree. Perhaps with this release I could qualify as a composer.

I learned a great deal about the collecting of royalties after the creation of *Rivers from the Sun.* After the album's release in 2005, I joined the Music Genome Project. This is what Pandora uses to create their playlists. A list of other similar songs is constructed using what the company calls its "matching algorithm." I had no idea if they had even accepted *Rivers from the Sun.*

Years passed and occasionally someone would tell me that they heard a song of mine on Pandora. I didn't give it much notice. My digital distributor is CD Baby, and they did not have a relationship with Pandora, so I never saw any payments. Beginning in 2014, I was contacted by Sound Exchange (a company that collects Featured Artist and Artist Royalties) saying they thought I was due some royalties. I didn't really understand royalty collection at that point, so I did nothing about it. Then, in February of 2017, I got a call from Chris at Rident Royalties out of Austin Texas, and we talked for almost an hour. He convinced me to let them go after whatever I was due that they could collect. In July of that year, I received a check for $13,000, though they withheld another $5,000 for taxes. I was blown away! This represented going back three years, collecting only Featured Artist and Artist royalties. About that time, CD Baby started collecting for Mechanical plays and Publishing Royalties from Pandora as well. They only went back one year, but I received another nice lump sum. I was also encouraged to join the American Society of Composers, Authors and Publishers (ASCAP). I very recently got an Artist Management Page or AMP on Pandora. The first time I opened my page I discovered I have had over 20.8 million lifetime streams on Pandora and currently am on 1300 Stations. That is just amazing. My plays on Spotify are next to nothing. That reveals how significant the algorithms and resulting playlists are in who gets heard.

My relationship with ASCAP and BMI was sketchy at best. For years I would start a decent gig at a restaurant or winery and eventually ASCAP would find out the place had bands performing and demand a sum of money to pay for covers being played. This would often end the live music in that establishment. This happened more than once. I didn't think of ASCAP as a friend, but then they do collect songwriter royalties that are another stream I was due to receive. I joined them and got another check.

Through all this I received an education about where royalties come from and how to collect them as a songwriter. I then contacted many of my songwriter friends who had released albums and not one was aware of these five streams of revenue that need to be addressed when you release an album. The five paying streams associated with every streaming play are Featured Artist, Artist, Mechanical, Publishing, and Songwriter Royalties. They are all miniscule, but if you are getting any number of plays, they can pile up. I continue to get somewhere around 100K plays a month on Pandora and am very grateful that Chris enlightened me about what I was due. Mechanical Plays are paid monthly. The other royalties are all paid quarterly. I encourage any songwriters to make sure they understand this process, as streaming has replaced CDs as the prominent way music is listened to in 2023.

Another angle for songs to create revenue is the release of videos. I haven't made very many, but they have been fun to produce and get a little attention. Mostly, I have strung together photographs that match the feel of the music with many songs on *Rivers from the Sun* and posted them to YouTube. While visiting my daughter, Dolphin, and her family in Alaska,

I took a lot of photos from the airplanes I had to hop on to get to her place in the wilds. Those photos accompany my most successful song to date, *Eagle Flies at Dawn*. I also met a wonderful man while stuck in the Anchorage airport on my return trip. Heeouk Park is from South Korea and traveled to many countries to bicycle for months at a time. He chronicled his journey with photographs that were incredible. We conversed for much of the time while we endured a 12-hour delay, and he told me of his travels. I used his photos, with his permission, from a trip to Nepal and another trip from Syria to Egypt. They accompany the music from *Divinitys' Way* and *Mediterranean Dream* on YouTube. We have stayed in touch, and he continues to travel when possible.

There are other videos on YouTube from live performances with the various duos and bands I have played with. Sadly, the 15 years with the original Grace Note occurred before the time of cell phones, with cameras at everyone's disposal.

Dancing in Relationship

In 2005, I also released the album *Dance When Your Soul Brings You Near*. Its composition took about six months working with Skip Brown and the many musicians I invited into the studio. For this album, I first played all the piano tracks with drummer Randy Anders, and then added additional tracks as desired. It is a rich album, with many different styles of music. I still play many of the songs for live gigs on occasion. The basic theme of most of the songs on this album is my relationship with women. The title track is both an invitation and an invocation to the richness and mystery of being in a relationship.

Dance When Your Soul Brings You Near

Reaching out, taking a chance to discover
Talk to me. Help me break down my cover
There is no map to guide us
No trail in the dark
Only the light made by sparks brought on by kindness
With nothing to fear dance when your soul brings you near

Moving slow patience gives birth to the moment
Afterglow respect for the rising serpent
Where there is peace there is love
The caged bird turns into a dove
Only the depths of true mercy are earned in forgiveness
With nothing to fear dance when your soul brings you near

Turning 'round spirit is at the beginning
Silent sound, how can we hear what we're saying
Live in the pause there is more in between
The dark and the light than is ever seen
Watching my heart prepare for this understanding
With nothing to fear dance when your soul brings you near

Dance with the moon and the stars, dance under open skies
Dance in the morning dew, dance with the fireflies
Dance with a warm embrace, dance under rising grace
Dance with a smile in your eyes, dance and enjoy the surprise
Dance when your soul, dance when your soul
Dance When Your Soul Brings You Near

I have been blessed to live with six different women in what would be called romantic partnerships, two of them marriages. I know I have learned much about myself and this world by being in these relationships as well as from the many relationship attempts, starting from a very young age.

My first encounter with strong feelings for the female side of our equation came when I was only seven years old for a classmate in second grade. I suspect most people refer to these encounters as infatuation, but I know to me it was a very real feeling I was experiencing. There was no attempt at communication, and I doubt the girl ever knew what I was feeling, but my parents did know and that resulted in some unexpected trauma.

Each Christmas we had these joke presents that were shared around the dinner table before the big meal. I remember the joke on me was that I had a girlfriend except I didn't, and I left the table in tears. Later I would discover that the message I got from that encounter was that my parents didn't believe I could love someone else. That one hurt, so on to the next infatuation, and this one lasted much longer.

In third grade I found myself enamored with another classmate, Peg. This again would go unrequited, and I doubt she even knew what I was feeling, but the feelings persisted year after year. I finally fessed up in my senior year in high school. She in the most gracious manner, at least recognized me and we shared some communication about the "situation." She had pretty much always had other boyfriends from the seventh grade on, which left the door closed for me. She met her husband-to-be from a nearby high school that senior year. They are still together, and she made a very wise choice of partners. They have created a beautiful family, and both had careers they enjoyed in as stable an environment as hoped for in these times. Stability in the culturally accepted sense hasn't exactly been my forte. At that time, I could not shake my feelings for her or even substitute someone else. I dreamt about her quite a bit until I was in my 40s and I did some therapy. It seemed that we may have been together in a past life. Acknowledging that possibility loosened up my attachments. We remain friends to this day, and I am grateful for her trust and steadfastness in that friendship.

My other experiences of "dating" in high school were what might be called coming-of-age experiences. By my senior year I still had not kissed a girl. I was cast into our senior play with a part where I had to kiss a girl in the story. I was determined that would not be my first kiss! I purposely dated another classmate hoping I could at last get a kiss goodnight and voilà, it happened. Soon after, the floodgates opened. I did not have a car, but my parents at least lent me their car occasionally for extracurricular activities. My summer after graduating was basically work and fun. And then on to college!

One might expect that college would become a lovefest of sorts for me, but that wasn't the reality. I developed several close friendships and had brief encounters, but nothing materialized of a deep connection until the very end of my freshman year. Into my life walked Claire and making love for the first time. She had just graduated and was moving on, and I was getting ready to fly to California to work in a church sponsored program for the summer. I suspect part of what allowed this to happen was because it was safe in a way of no long-term commitments for us both. Our intimacy expanded over the course of several days. What we created was a breakthrough for me. I literally had to be coached during our first night together. Her patience and love were enduring and empowering. So, I headed off to California, having just been defrocked.

If my parents knew what they had signed me up for with that church program, I have no doubt they would have pulled the plug. My arrival in San Diego was ten days before the Greater Parish Ministries program I was to work for started. There was a workshop scheduled for the weekend after I arrived which I was encouraged to attend. The subject was sexuality. I had no clue what I was getting into but went in as the youngest person there (ages from myself at 19 to upper 70s.) There were about 40 of us gathered at a church. Once there, we were ushered into a large basement room where there were sheets hanging on the walls and projectors positioned all over the room. After we settled in the lights went down and a movie started with a man and woman making love. Then a second projector with two men and a third with two women and then slides of all manner of sexual encounters. This went on for 15-20 minutes. The lights then came up and a person dressed as a minister stood at one end of the room while two people advanced from the other, looking as if they were to be married. The minister character then said, *"I now pronounce you man and woman."* My mind was blown at that point, to say the least.

The weekend continued with us visiting the Marine Corps training base, meeting with some Black Panther representatives, visiting the nightlife on the streets, and finally sharing a wonderful meal together in an old airplane hangar that an artist had converted into his studio. The meal was served on the floor in a long line of food that we sat around. There was no silverware, and we were asked not to feed ourselves but to feed each other. The symbolism was profound for me at that time.

The program itself began shortly after, and I worked with inner city black children for the remainder of the summer, but the fireworks continued in other departments. The first family I was assigned to live with was a young couple. He was in the Navy and away at sea at the time, and she invited me into her bedroom the second night I was there. Remember this is 1969, the summer of love and I reckon it was contagious. Needless to say, when her husband returned there were some fireworks of a different kind and after an evening where we talked through the entire scene in a very positive way, with the managers of the program present, it was decided that I would move in with the big wigs for the rest of the summer.

Another development of that summer was my introduction to mind altering drugs. I had not smoked marijuana at that point, nor consumed anything resembling psychedelics. At the invitation of the young man who ran our program at the church I consumed some organic mescaline. I then proceeded to get high while swimming in the Pacific Ocean. I remember the quality of experience being dominated by the recognition of a sense of unity within all things. We later returned to his apartment and listened to music with the song *Celebrate* by Three Dog Night setting the tone. It was a remarkable day to say the least. This opened the door to exploring various psychedelics for a few years. Ultimately it propelled me into a worldview dominated by the discovery of consciousness as the prime channel for humanities and my own development or growth.

The remainder of my time at Earlham and the next few years in and out of Boston, my relationships with women were often surprising, warm, and most often friendships. There were a few love affairs and I continued to learn about attachment and letting go. My journals from this time were full of references to my desire for a relationship and not knowing how to proceed except to trust the divine.

My friendship with Stephanie is typical of what transpired for me during this time. I have had a longtime habit of spending time in trees. I find it exhilarating and challenging at the same time. One day, while sitting in a tree in the Fens, (a park area near Queensbury St) a young woman passed me by and greeted me with an enthusiastic *"Hi!"* This led me to climb down and catch up to her, pursuing conversation. Conversation led to her apartment and onward, and after two weeks we went on as friends. I introduced her to Ken Shaw, a musician friend, and they took to each other with a magical, explorative attitude. They shared a close relationship for the next two years. Meanwhile, she and I remained in touch. She visited me a few times while living at Birdsfoot Farm. Many years later, whenever I was doing craft fairs in the D.C. area, I would stay with her and her family in Georgetown. Our friendship grew, though when her family had to sell her house on Old Georgetown Road, sometime after 2000, I eventually lost contact, as so often happens in this mobile society we are a part of. Relationships that have been meaningful for me have often extended themselves through the following decades. For this I am very grateful.

So, as I am writing this today, a few days ago I was contacted by Stephanie and her husband Perry. They were traveling south and decided to stay overnight in Floyd and see if they could find me. They chose to stay at the Pine Tavern Lodge which is managed by a bass playing friend of mine, David Owens. He put them in touch with me and we visited until 12 that night. I had written the above paragraph just three weeks before. Again, I am reminded how incredible this universe is and how lucky and grateful I am to maintain meaningful relationships.

There have been women I have lived with for extended periods of time. There have also been periods of time in between relationships. As I grew older those in-between times were mixed in nature, often challenging and often very creative, emphasizing my introspective character that shows up in the lyrics of many songs. A song about those in-between times, *Dusty Pillow*, kicks off the album *Dance When Your Soul Brings You Near*. It is a lighthearted look at such times.

Dusty Pillow

Dusty pillow laying on my bed
It's not the one waiting for my head, it's waiting for you, waiting for you
Book of poems that I ain't read
Songs to write but I ain't dared, they're waiting for you, waiting for you
    Slowly the moon rises over my head
    Looks like a friend tonight
    I hear the hoot owl singing his song
    Saying who, who are you

Winter, summer, spring and fall
They each are different, but I love them all
While waiting for you, waiting for you
Bottle of wine labeled 92
It's getting better, it's the natural thing to do
While waiting for you, waiting for you
    Softly the clouds drift in the sky
    Looking like friends I've known
    Some I remember, some I let go
    Saying who, who are you

I probably ask too many questions

I keep feeling the great tides
A star is falling in slow motion
Saying who who who who who are you?

What are the energies that bring us together? I have shared in many conversations about the qualities of mutual attraction or repulsion. Do we notice hair color, smell, looks, sound of voice, height, weight, color of eyes, skin, before we notice how anyone makes us feel in their presence? How much of attraction is simple hormones and pheromones? I once participated in a conversation with a group of friends who were all in couples. Someone asked the question of how long after you met did you make love the first time? Turns out, three days or less was the answer for everyone except me. I was then married to Jayn, and it was close to six weeks for us. Perhaps that was a precursor to the struggles I would encounter in our relationship.

There are perhaps many more esoteric ideas about what brings us together as well. Past lives together and soul contracts are concepts that get some attention. Finding your soulmate seems to be an exercise for many, perhaps a futile ideal and more likely a claim we should make about everyone we encounter, as it would make it more likely we would see the good in each other daily.

As a young person, I never imagined that I would be in so many relationships with women. I was brought up like so many of us are, with the idea that one marriage was the ideal and sought-after path forward. My parents lived that example, and as far as I could tell they were fairly happy with their arrangement.

My early relationships were characterized by passion and indecision, leading to breakups from both sides of the relationship. The time in between was a blessing of freedom and growth. I once wrote that my ideal life would be freedom in insecurity, as it would constantly point me toward stretching my understanding of what it is to be here. In the realm of sexual activity, I grew to understand that I wanted to have a positive experience of sex and not condemn myself or others for sex outside of marriage. A series of past life regressions reinforced this attitude.

I was regressed by a friend of Katie's who visited us for two weeks on Birdsfoot farm. Donna asked me what issue I wanted to explore and what came up was my sexuality. In the first regression I was a young girl on a Viking ship. My sole purpose was to sex and cook for the men. I threw myself overboard, making sex feel pretty wrong. My second regression involved being a woman in the 1700's, in my mid-30's, and married to a man who physically and sexually abused me. Despite having two children, I fell down some stairs and didn't try to end my fall, thus dying from the injury. This was another extreme way to escape sex. Finally, I discovered myself living during the gold rush in California and finding "true love" at a young age. After three years of being together she suddenly died. (perhaps in childbirth) I couldn't handle the thought of that kind of loss again, so I joined a monastery. Again dodging sex. I realized I wanted to find a way to enjoy sex in this life and not continue to make it wrong or pretend it didn't matter as a life force.

As a result of being regressed I decided to offer this process to a few friends. I found I could be present with whomever was regressing in a way that allowed them to discover a path forward through whatever issues were being highlighted. Over the years I have done over 400 of them for folks and witnessed some incredible events. Two individuals I regressed described the same experience of Atlantis going down in a huge catastrophe. They did not know each other, and the regressions were 10 years apart. Most folks lived rather simple lives complicated by relationships and the suffering humanity seems to be capable of inflicting on each other. I feel blessed to have witnessed this window into so many people's lives and souls with the trust they offered me in sharing their intimate journeys. Stephen W. wrote of his experience, *"I got more out of it than I could have expected. It was profound. Much more fun than algebra. My experience with Bob was a major step in my spiritual journey of discovering who I am, and I will be forever grateful for his help."*

The experience of finding myself in a woman's body during a regression also stretched my compassion for the female experience in this lifetime. As I moved into doing regressions for other people, and as I became friends with many women throughout this life, it was apparent that sexual abuse is rampant in Western Civilization and other cultures. Too many women have shared intimate stories about sufferings at the hands of fathers, uncles, or men invited into their homes when they were children. Healing these wounds is a pathway necessary, it seems, for all of us to acknowledge in order for the violence that is so rampant to abate.

Jayn and I came together to have children, as I have described, and the years of our marriage were characterized by many ups and downs as we struggled to find a way forward that fit both of us. Our care for our children never faded, and it remained a sound foundation for our time together.

The fact we got married was more of a burden to Jayn than a welcomed reality. I asked her to marry me months before my dad died, as I wanted to share with him he was going to be a grandfather and that we were married, which I knew was important to him. Jayn agreed, but only if we had an open marriage. The following years led to emotional stretches on both our parts as we lived out that reality. My father passed less than two months after we shared the news that he was to become a grandparent. Sadly, he never got to meet his first grandchild.

I lived as a partner with Jayn for 18 years. I remain in community at Zephyr with her still. Our continued acceptance and presence around each other are a tremendous gift. We have always been friends. That was a basis for our relationship, but the sexual angle was difficult for her to express and for me to accept the lack of. I had several affairs, most of them non-threatening to our relationship. Only twice during that time did I feel the call to perhaps move on. The first time ended when Linda B. requested a stop to our meeting because she did not want me to lose my relationship with my children. This had been precisely what had happened to her with her only son and thankfully she spared me that fate. The second relationship was much closer to home.

A friend and I felt drawn to each other during the year of the harmonic convergence. She was separated from her husband and what ensued between us eventually forced me to choose between her and Jayn. With many twists and turns, I eventually asked Jayn to stay in relationship with me, but to let the relationship become monogamous. I wrote this poem during this time with this friend in mind.

Oldest Friend

Were you my oldest friend?
Were you living when I came to be born again?
Spotted me out of the corner of your eye
A glance, only to return to your play
This dream has begotten a bold look

A chance to recover our instinct
As if a mountain climb would make us bolder
We stand at the cliffs' base naked within the dream
Our only tools faith, trust and patience
Reaching together for places quickening with aliveness
Knowing the hand feels the grasp as the rock extends
Life expands like drum rolls in a canyon
We echo each other's divinity
When you were my oldest friend, our bones ached
A small sacrifice for the seat closest to the fire
We are not clever, there is nothing to defeat
We come to hold the baton the Master leaves each sunrise

The trust and love we share has deepened with time, and I have much gratitude for the many conversations, shared rituals, meals, and growth we have facilitated by continued acceptance of each other's presence. The song, *Release Me*, was written during this era of my life. *Release Me* features Billy Bell's saxophone and appears on both *Circles Returning* and *Rewind*.

Release Me

Release me, oh release me to live in trust I am worthy Release me.
Release me, oh release me into the stars I want to fly oh release me
Release me, oh release me to laugh and cry to live or die release me

Refrain:
   From the mother to the sun, we are children we are one
   If the lessons are not learned empty nothing we return
   To live and die, I want to fly oh release me.

After years of both closeness and distress (and several attempts at therapy together), on my 44th birthday I awoke and realized the biggest gift I could give myself was to move on from living with Jayn. I took my dresser and clothes and moved into my 10ft by 16ft music studio that I had built just down the driveway from the farmhouse. At first, I wasn't at all sure I could remain at Zephyr, or how any of this was going to proceed. But as the days and months unfolded, it seemed I could remain welcomed in Jayn's presence and move forward on my own. I continued to work with her on the pottery for another 3 years. We found friendship to be much easier than marriage.

Our divorce proceedings were actually very easy and simple. We accomplished our separation without the help of a lawyer. The only complicated thing for me was getting my birth name back. We had merged our names in marriage to become Avery-Grubel. My first 4 recordings all have my name as Bob Avery-Grubel on the cover. After the divorce agreement was accepted in court, Jayn's name reverted to her birth name without any legal maneuvers. I had to go to the County Clerk with my birth certificate and other ID, then pay 12 bucks to get my name back. I imagine it would cost a whole lot more now!

Staying nearby also gave me proximity to my children, who were 14 and 17 at the time. When it became clear this was the way forward, my younger daughter exclaimed, "We knew this would happen. What took you so long?" It wasn't until June of that year that I was both certain I wanted to remain at Zephyr and then given permission by the group to expand my studio into a livable home space. I spent most of that summer building a two-room addition to the studio that resulted in a 600 square foot home and a start on a new path forward.

The building of this home was accomplished largely with wood from trees I dropped here at Zephyr, and then had bandsaw milled. Each addition I made to my home was done this way. One big exception was finding 2000 pieces of plywood cutoffs (as they were 10 inches by 4 feet cut from full sheets of plywood) that came from a nearby mill for 10 cents apiece. This amounted to a 4ft by 8ft sheet of half-inch plywood for under a dollar. I used these pieces for siding on the entire house and it has held up very well over the years. I also timbered some walnut from my friend Lee Stone's home which accented the inside windows and floors.

Expanding my studio to become a welcoming home

Through the next several years I had a few relationships that cemented the idea there was no going back to Jayn. I also discovered that the women I attracted didn't feel my 600 square foot abode was offering a space that interested them. In the summer of 1997, I began building the largest addition to my studio home with the mantra *"if you build it, she will come"* humming in my head. Shortly after, Dee arrived in my life.

Dee and I shared an on-again, off-again 4 years. There was a great deal of attraction between us, and we had many fun adventures together. She had a deep interest in animal welfare and brought my second dog, Prairie, into my life. Despite the good we shared, I struggled with accepting some of her preferences and limitations. After we had separated, Dee and I went to an auction where she bid on a house and one acre of land. With my encouragement she made one final offer and got the bid. She still resides in that beautiful home today. As with many of my love relationships, we remain close friends to this day, and I have witnessed a tremendous amount of growth in her personal life as she navigates her way forward. I wrote the song *Something About It* with Dee's presence in mind.

Something About It

Must be something about it, something about the way you talk
Something about it, something about the way you walk
Something about it, something about the look in your eyes
I'm not surprised to notice how gentle you are
When others would keep on walking
You reach for the scar and you're healing

Must be something about it, something about the time of day
Something about it, something about the silver and grey
Something about it, something about the sacred way
When nothing is missing right here and there's always enough
And when you breathe in with me
I'm blown thru the top by your healing

The world is a welcome place, she gives all we are
I've seen it in rivers flowing with sparkling stars
There's something about it

There's something about it, something about the letting go

Something about it, something about the dancing flow
Something about it, something about the space in between
Daylight and darkest midnight, the threshold of dreams
Hold onto what is gathering
And what we bring to this healing

Must be something about it, something about the way we are
Something about it, something about the look in your eyes
Something about it, something about the way we are

As my relationships evolved, I found myself writing songs that mirrored some experiences I was living. At this juncture in my life, I wrote many songs and poetry about the intensity of my emotional space. Two songs that kind of summed up that moment of meeting until more is discovered are *Love is Like a Mirror* and *I Am Amazed*.

Love Is Like a Mirror

Well I can't stop thinking about you baby
And we ain't even made love yet
Well I can't stop thinking about you cause I don't want to forget
Everywhere I go everything I see, I keep thinking you're the one for me
I know it's kinda silly to feel such a way
I might as well risk it cause it's happening anyway
Keep on telling me what you need to say
I want to hear your heart speaking everyday
    Love is like a mirror showing me my heart

Can't make no assumptions baby, this song is all I got
Can't know about tomorrow honey, that's the good Lord's lot
When I see the moonrise over the hill
Brings me back to your eyes it's such a thrill
    Love is like a mirror showing me my heart

You sit down with me and you touch me with your thigh
I wonder if you notice when I'm ready to cry
Cry about the passion that flames and then dies
Love is something else I'm ready to try
    Love is like a mirror, showing me my heart

I Am Amazed was written shortly after I met my second wife through actual marriage, Cate G. She and I met online and began a long-distance relationship that we both enthusiastically embraced. She was a resident of St. Simon's Island, Georgia, and a lifelong lover of the ocean with a degree in marine biology. The trek back and forth was 7 ½ hours of driving. Four months after we met, she made the move to the mountains of Virginia to share this home with me. We continued to travel back and forth frequently, as her son was then a senior in high school and engaged in activities that she and I wanted to support. St. Simons is also just a great place to be, offering a big contrast to the mountains particularly in the winter months.

Cate was a muse for me and during my time with her, and after, I wrote many songs, including finishing the album *Rivers from the Sun*. The song, *I Am Amazed,* is as close to a country song as I will ever write.

I Am Amazed

I can't stop thinking about you
I feel your heart reaching my way
Your smile is right here inside me, and I am amazed

Your red hair flows like an angel
The wind blows sparks my way
I breathe in light and remember I am amazed

    Chances are, the brightest star
    Is made up of love we're dreaming of together
    And I am amazed

Your laughter lifts my burden
Helps me see so clear
And when we touch I am certain I am amazed

    Baby I'm amazed, honey I'm amazed

Two other songs inspired early in our relationship were *I'm in You and You're In Me* and *Your Love*.

I'm In You and You're In Me

When your love came my way, I didn't know what to say
So the words just tumbled out in a rush
With my heart open like the sky by the look in your eyes
Now I'm learning to feel everything that is real
And it's passing back and forth between us
The road is so wide when I'm riding by your side
Like the wave is the sea and the bird flies easily
I'm in you and you're in me

And we'll reach out our hands work to understand
Listen to the inner holy hush
When we're walking in the rain or sun, we are held by the one
The greatest mystery is doing what comes naturally
In the soft and steady presence of trust
Palm to palm and sigh to sigh we're clearing out the rust
Like the wave is the sea and the bird flies easily
I'm in you and you're in me

Watching grow, what we know letting go into forever

Now this love is here today and I'm so grateful come what may
I will sing this song as long as I'm alive
With you listening I'll sing out clear
With you by my side I'll have no fear
Like the wave is the sea and the bird flies easily
I'm in you and you're in me.

Your Love

Your love is making me higher than I ever dreamed I would go
Your love is lighting this fire and I know it will surely grow
Every time you look my way, I see your blue eyes widen
Your kisses hanging in the air make me feel like I'm in heaven
With your love

Your love shines like the full moon, the glow has opened my heart
Your love it didn't come on to soon, it felt right from the start
I'm so grateful every day for all the twists and turns

That brought you to my doorstep so I could finally learn about heaven
In your love

Several watershed moments marked Cate's time living with me at Zephyr. Fairly soon after arriving here, she determined she was really not into living in a community such as it was. After much discussion, we felt we might move on to another location together, so we looked for another place to live and I put my home on the market. We found a house that Martin Scudder, my violin partner from Grace Note, and his father were interested in selling and made moves in that direction. For a while it looked as though it would actually happen. I built a sizable outside storage building and did some repairs on the new location. Then we finally sat down with Martin's dad and wife to finalize the agreement. As we drove away from that encounter, we looked at each other and both said that we should not do this. Changing our minds about that meant staying at Zephyr and it also led to a falling-out between Martin and I that ended his time playing with Grace Note. This is one of the few times in my life I regret not pausing more before my conversations with him and his dad. We both pitched a fit and thus it was several years before we played music together again. He has since played on several of my albums, and we are on good terms as friends once again. Time seems to heal all wounds, given the chance. Forgiving self and others widens the path as well.

Cate and I both shared a deep interest in many different healing modalities. I had discovered deep tissue massage and past life regressions years before. Cate was interested in energy work having attained Levels 1 and 2 in Reiki. My lifelong friend, Lee Stone, was a Reiki Master, and we engaged in his class, after which Cate attained Master status. Cate took to the work like a fish to water and it became a basis for her healing work going forward. I added it to my repertoire as well. She continues with this work to this day.

After Martin's place fell through, Cate agreed to keep on at Zephyr. But the following spring she felt it necessary to check out living somewhere else. On May 5th, 2006, Cate drove down the driveway, and I have not seen her since. We remain in touch, and I recognize a strong heart connection still, without the need for physical presence. The song *Without Tomorrow* summed up my experience, as this relationship changed and ultimately led to a divorce that fall. I perform this song often and frequently get comments on the truth it shares about being here as relationships change.

Without Tomorrow

Hardly got to know you and you were gone
Everything about you was moving on
Seems there was a chance for us to grow
But then no one really knows
About tomorrow only today, oh tomorrow

Writing this song makes me churn inside
The memories burning and I can't hide
Everyone says May will turn to June
Even when you're standing on the dark side of the moon
Dreaming of tomorrow when there's only today, oh tomorrow

She blew a kiss, I thought what's this, what's this?
How do you take what hurts so bad
And turn it into honoring the good you had
Going to the river just fits my soul
Wash away the teardrops til I am whole
Without tomorrow, only today, oh tomorrow
    Hardly got to know you and you were gone....

There are two other songs from the album *Dance When Your Soul Brings You Near* that speak of the challenges in relationships. While listening to Leonard Cohen's music, I found permission to write *Aching Blue*.

Aching Blue

I've busted my heart open with the calling and repeat
Who can really prosper on that edge
Looking at the wooded places sounds from echoes feet
Masking sweetness in this cool embrace

I've lied because I could not find a way to see the truth
Hurting really lays its hand on me
Like seventy blind puppets dancing on their strings
Who controls the thoughts of destiny

> I've been looking back now I'm broken too
> What I hold too tight just fades away

Some golden image always plays just around the bend
I don't want to look there anymore
I'm digging in the dirt to find a different kind of friend
I'm falling off the bridge between the shores
> I've been looking back now I'm broken too
> What I hold too tight just slips away

Voices come from everywhere what am I to do
Silence has a ring inside it too
Like broadcast news the words rampage until they're aching blue
Do it tune them out or dare to feel them through
> I've been looking back thinking about you
> And I find I'm aching blue
> I've been looking back now I'm broken too
> If I hold too tight, I'm aching blue

Another song I enjoy performing with guest musicians or solo is *Making Shadows Out of Me*. It is a bluesy tune that many listeners have commented on over the years and it asks how we get relief or soothing when things are rough. Having burned wood to heat my homes for the past 50 years, it is appropriate that there is more than just heat emerging from those many beautiful flames.

Making Shadows Out of Me

I got no fix for these cheap tricks
Life keeps on throwing my way
It's quite a pickle but it's not dull
It's been quite a day

I got no charms they've all been disarmed
Most of them sent out to sea
But when I'm able I pick up the cost
Send the bill to me

> Sometimes it's just got to be
> Some folks call it destiny

Sacks full of rain fall on my roof
And it's not even my property
So I'll sit by the fire and listen for free
It's making shadows out of me

The time after Cate left provided some miracle moments—affirming the support that is waiting in each moment. Cate and I agreed that if I gave her $2000 that would be sufficient to release us from the marriage documents. I had no idea where the money would come from, but in less than 2 weeks it manifested, and the divorce happened later in the fall.

While attending FloydFest that summer I met Sherry, and my next relationship was soon underway. Sherry enjoyed her time at Zephyr and grew close to the other members of the community while living here. We also discovered some connections from my past. While I was attending a high school choir reunion, I struck up a conversation with Terry (a basketball teammate from high school years) who lived on Long Island where Sherry was from. When I shared with him her name, his face lit up. Terry worked for many years with her mom, so he knew her family very well. Sometimes the tightness of this universe can be a wonderful reminder of how connected we all are.

Another mutual acquaintance was a friend known as the Barefoot Farmer, Jeff Poppen. He and I had met many years before through the folks who shared their candle making skills with me. Jeff hosted a weekend workshop on his farm in Tennessee each fall focused on biodynamic teachings. Jeff's farm is amazing, and his gardens are among the most fruitful I have ever seen. He has written books and lectured on his organic growing techniques. He is very worthy of adding to anyone's garden guru list!

Sherry and I also practiced Tai Chi together, as it was offered at the Chinese Medicine Clinic in Floyd. This was one of those times when the form I originally learned from Benjamin Lo re-entered my life.

Our time together was characterized by an easy warmth and care for each other. We enjoyed each other's families and friends and for a while it looked and felt as though we were headed for as many years together as life would grant us. As it happens, life had other plans!

In the late fall of 2009, Sherry was looking for a new job. In December, she had an interview in Louisville, KY. At the same time, I had an interview with a woman who was interested in my vocalizing skills and workshops for her nonprofit, Circle Toward Wholeness. This was Sandy Jahmi Burg, and my life was about to change in ways I only imagined possible.

When I first arrived at Sandy's doorstep and the door opened, I had an instant recognition. *This is the person you have waited your whole life to be with.* I knew right then what lay ahead would be interesting, challenging and ultimately as rewarding as life can offer. We immediately began an enthusiastic discussion with all manner of possibilities being shared. During the evening, Sherry called from Louisville and told me she got the job. She asked if I wanted to move to Louisville with her and all I could say at the moment was that we could talk about it. My heart knew something else was afoot.

Two nights after we met, Sandy had a dream that I was also the one she was looking for. This—combined with an established understanding that the person she would be partnered with would live a simpler lifestyle—opened her to a different kind of exploration. As we exchanged emails, it became apparent that our next meeting would be about more than business. We agreed to get together again near the end of December to see what this really was about.

When we met again, as we shared our life's stories, it became apparent we could create a life together. It wasn't long before we both realized we wanted to give this new relationship a chance to flourish. During this second evening, getting to know each other affirmed our connection and set the wheels in motion for me to end my relationship, as it was, with Sherry.

The return home that evening began three understandably difficult days of sharing with Sherry. I did my best to be available to the questions, concerns, pain of loss, letting goes, anticipations and joys, all wrapped into my experience as the year ended. Sherry, and many of my friends and family, were quite pissed at me! All I could offer was my understanding that something else was happening that needed patience and allowing to be revealed. This was a moment of deep trust in the twists and turns of life and my commitment to honoring what I feel and sense through my awareness or intuition. There was also an understanding of how the many changes in relationships, until this moment, had prepared me to accept the criticisms and stand in my truth. Sherry and I resolved a path forward that meant I needed to stay in other places until she could leave for Louisville at the end of February. This was fine with me, and I ended up staying with the Giessler's at Zephyr or with Sandy.

Once again, my birthday was a date with added significance. Sandy visited Zephyr for the first time on the eve of my birthday and woke up her first morning in what would be her home by mid-April on my birthday. I handled the transition between these two beautiful women in the best manner I could create at the time. I am now 13 years with Sandy, and Sherry has been with her found love for over 10 years. Somehow, what fits has arrived for all of us. My gratitude for Sandy's presence is expressed every day and her expressions of gratitude for me are a most welcome addition to the beating of my heart. I will share much more about my time with Sandy later, when my song for Sandy arrives!

Music and dance have always had an interplay that lifts both the dancer and the musician. All over the world these two energies merge to lift our spirits, invigorate our bodies and just plain bring people together. *Good Time Blues*, the eleventh track on *Dance When Your Soul Brings You Near,* honors that delightful experience. Joel Venditti played some excellent guitar on this track that encourages the listener to get up and shake your booty!

Good Time Blues

Hey baby you got your good time shoes on
Hey baby you got them good time shoes on
You look like you could dancing til the break of dawn

Hey baby you got them good time clothes on
Hey baby you got them good time threads on
You look like you could go strolling on and on and on
 When bad times come a knocking it's hard to do your best
 But good times leave you laughing and ready for the rest

Hey baby you got your time wings on
Hey baby you got your pretty feathers on
You look like you could go flying up to the stars and beyond

 Well hard times leave you crawling and laying on the floor
 While good times get you ready for rolling out the door

Hey baby you got your good time moves on
Hey baby you got them good time moves on
And I think I am ready come on come on

There are three women who have shared my life at Zephyr for many years. Katherine has made a unique and substantial contribution to my life. She is a very knowledgeable herbalist and has taught many people about the varied uses of herbs. For many years, she shared her wisdom at our local health food store, The Harvest Moon. She has unfolded a life rich in ritual, prayer and poetry. At our equinox gatherings, she often led the opening of ceremonies we shared. She also raised her five sons mostly by herself, which demonstrated the strength of her character and commitment to them. I am sure my life would be very different without our many conversations and the contributions she has made regarding health and inner dynamics.

Jody Franko has been one of my biggest teachers about acceptance and my judgments. She married Tom here at Zephyr on the Fall Equinox in 1985. Early in our relationship we butted heads often about things which I have no memories of now. I found myself distancing myself from her for no good reason in those moments. At some point, I made a conscious choice to pay attention to the many positive things she brought into her life. She is an amazing, committed mom to her twin daughters. She was a major player in creating our land trust agreement, for which I am most thankful. Her abundant enthusiasm could be contagious when I opened to it. As I paid attention to her in those ways, our relationship shifted and now there is as much room for sharing and trust as there is with anyone I may know.

Diane came to the farm in the mid late '80s with her husband, Dick. She has a steady, calm presence that inspires confidence and trust in those around her. She and Dick worked for the same developmental disabilities support organization that I did for many years, the only difference being they took residents into their home full time. I worked for them for over a decade, always grateful for their direction and support in the work I performed. They hosted many gatherings and meetings in their beautiful home. They chose to leave Zephyr for a home closer to Floyd in 2014. Dick passed last year after 5 years of dealing with a series of strokes. Diane and Dick's daughter, Lora Leigh, maintained a caring presence for Dick during his decline. Particularly in the last 2 years, as she and Diane brought him out of a local nursing home and did most of his care themselves. I visit Diane occasionally and she returns to Zephyr for shared ceremony and meals often. Our conversations always feel like fruit plucked from the vine, ripened and sweet.

There have also been many significant men in my life beyond members of my family. In the mid 1980's, I met a man who would become a mentor in my musical life. Jan (pronounced *Yawn*) Oosting was an incredible presence, standing well over 6ft tall and over 300lbs. He was the pianist for the Raleigh Symphony Orchestra at the age of twelve. His musical skills were amazing, as he played at least ten different instruments, and he had many other skills as well. In an interview for a local paper about him, they quoted me as saying *"He's one of the more talented people I've ever met. In the world of music, he's mastered as many instruments as many folks could master in many lives. He's a good carpenter, too, a hell of a carpenter."* He played professional football for 2 seasons, as a lineman for the Detroit Lions. Unfortunately, his left hand got messed up in that employment and could never perform on piano as well after that (he was still amazing). I often shared my songs with him as I wrote them, and he would critique them for me. He gave me many ideas about composition and was always encouraging me. Jan died in 2008 of congestive heart failure. The value of his mentoring has remained though the rest of my life.

Another longtime friend, Arthur Swers, lives within one mile of my home at Zephyr. Arthur is a lover of music and not a performer. Our friendship includes a love of baseball, many philosophical discussions, and the simple lifestyle we share. Arthur was my first sounding board when I was working on recordings. He would listen to what I had produced and give me honest feedback that was much appreciated.

Leaf Salem is a man whose poetic fever has lasted a lifetime. He and I have conversed on average every two weeks via the phone since his departure from Floyd some 20 years ago. I couldn't say that he influenced my music directly, but his philosophical dexterity certainly challenged and informed me over the years of our acquaintance. His wife, Lynn, died three years ago after 52 years of marriage. I had plane tickets to go visit him in Tucson, Arizona at the end of March 2020, but then Covid hit, and the flight never happened. These days I am less inclined to fly, so our getting together will likely remain over the phone or Zoom.

There are many other men who have remained friends over the decades of my life. This culture has allowed us so much mobility that they are scattered all across the country and in a few cases, the world. I have remained in contact as best I can, as it is important to me to embody the value of those relationships as we learn about living this life together. I am often surprised by the many creative endeavors and challenges faced by these friends and would hope that my presence in their lives has added some meaning as well.

During the 1990s, I organized a monthly men's group that met for over a decade, mostly in my home. Two books we read as a group were Robert Bly's *Iron John* and Michael Meade's *Men and the Waters of Life*. We often had very rich discussions and occasionally ended our meetings with a sauna. We took part in a few Talent Night fund- raisers by rewriting the lyrics to popular songs and performing them. Titles like "The Smells of Science" (*Sound of Silence*), "Funky Junky Car" (*Achy Breaky Heart*) and "The Floyd Reality" (*Yellow Submarine*) flowed out of our collective fun-seeking consciousness. The group was never any bigger than ten in number, but it provided a steady opportunity for those who came to share in a safe and supportive environment.

One comment of Robert Bly's that has stuck in my consciousness was the idea that one should not give away their gold before the age of 35. By "gold" he is referring to a person's creative gift. This is very contrary to the current popular music scene where the younger the person, the better, as far as the music "industry" is concerned. This emphasis on young, so-called talent leaves the industry in charge of people's lives. Success is largely defined in terms of numbers and the reality of a life lived with meaning and purpose is made more difficult in the glare of the lights. This youth-centered culture may be what many need, but I am uncertain that it will endure. I did not begin recording until I was 37, and Bly's observation bore fruit for me as prior years gave me many different experiences and insights to craft songs about, as well as to improve my musical skills.

Over the span of the last 40 years, I have been blessed to live with four remarkable men here at Zephyr—Ray Chantal, Tom Franko, Dick Giessler, and Perrin Heartway. Ray had a warmth of character that oozed out of his smile. Dick was always extending a sincere interest in others' well-being. Tom has a steadfast resonance that can be amplified with edgy sarcasm at times. I never had a blood brother, but if anyone has ever lived that role for me it would be Tom Franko. These men have engaged me with as much integrity as I have experienced from anyone. Their companionship has been a gift in my life here at Zephyr. The man whose family took over the Giessler residence here at Zephyr, Perrin Heartway, has also extended a caring, inquisitive presence. In some ways he and his wife Jenny have become the torch bearers for the future of this community.

There was another experience in my life with several men that was a gift in very different ways. This was through a part-time job I had as a respite caregiver from 1998 until 2019. Floyd County is home to a company, Wall Residences, that oversees the placement of physically and mentally handicapped individuals into private homes. A neighbor of ours asked me if I would be interested in this kind of caregiving work as a backup worker for them. This allowed the primary caregivers an opportunity to be away from their responsibilities for part of a day or sometimes longer. I thought I would give it a try. I felt right at home with the individuals I provided care for, and I learned a great deal from sharing my life with them.

Early in my work through Wall Residences, I was with G bowling when something occurred that I have never forgotten. G became very excited if he made a spare or a strike, jumping up and down and shouting loudly. After this happened a few times, I went over to a man bowling on a nearby lane and apologized for G's behavior, saying *"I hope he isn't bothering you."* The man replied, *"Are you kidding. It's great to see someone as enthusiastic as he is!"* He opened my eyes and exposed how much I was still living in a world of stereotypes. The work with these individuals was often challenging and incredibly rewarding. I learned more than words can express about acceptance, and the many ways love manifests in each of us.

For many years I also got to play music with the folks in this program. I led an afternoon sing along that yielded many smiles and lots of good times. I often adjusted the songs we sang to make them easy to sing along and participate creatively with. An example of this was a version of *I've*

Been Working on the Railroad. We each took a turn and picked out a favorite food, transforming the verse for each person. Using G as an example it would go *"Someone's in the kitchen with G, someone's in the kitchen I know, someone's in the kitchen with G, cooking hamburgers and singing fee fi fiddly I oh fee fi fiddly I oh, fee fi fiddly I oh cooking up hamburgers!"*

The last three songs on *Dance When Your Soul Brings You Near* explore a different relationship narrative. Our relationship to the earth is manifested in so many ways every day we live. We are dependent on this planet for all our sustenance. Two men I have been privileged to know have given back so much in the way they have lived. Tom Franko (who shares Zephyr as his home with me and others) has planted over a million trees. Bruce B. (from my high school days whom I remain in touch with) returned to his roots and bought a place less than a mile from where he grew up. He purchased 30 acres that was entirely open fields. In the past 40 or so years he has reforested the entire 30 acres with a diverse population of trees and shrubbery that has created an abundant refuge for wildlife. I can only hope my care for our 30 acres at Zephyr has contributed a small balance to the wealth I have received from this land. I pray that restoring health to our planet might become a priority as the years pass by going forward. *This Beautiful World* is a song that simply celebrates this mother earth we get to share the bounty of.

This Beautiful World

This beautiful world and all of its ways
I marvel at this, this song is in praise
This beautiful world, I'm lucky to see
And blessed by the light that's living in me

   Dance in the fountain, climb up the mountain (repeat)

This beautiful world, its' magical form
It whispers at night and screams in the storm
This beautiful world and all that I hear
The blessings of songs and silence is clear

   Dance in the moonlight, sing by the fireside (repeat)

Then there's the quiet place that lives in between
The laughter and holiness where pastures are green
Where pastures are green

This beautiful world around it goes
Creating the seasons, the dawn and the rose
This beautiful world, made before man
What spirit inspired by breath here I am

> *Dance hallelujah, this beautiful world will bless and serve you*
> *Dance hallelujah, this beautiful world, this beautiful world*

Accepting my inevitable mortality has been a process for me that in part involved the witnessing of many friends and loved ones passing through that door. My seven years as a hospice volunteer showed me much about how courageous and real some people become as their bodies wither away. There are times I am confronted daily with the loss of loved ones or the possibility of that occurring. For me, deaths seem to come in waves of at least three people over a period of months.

In 1999, I lost five friends, all of whom were in their late-40's or 50's. The first of these was a friend who was in prison for drug possession and facing a lengthy sentence. He committed suicide rather than remain imprisoned. Shortly after that, Zephyr lost its first founding father, Ray Chantal, in an unfortunate circumstance involving an ulcer and a hospital that turned him out in the middle of the night because he did not have insurance. He passed on two days later. The hospital was sued and the result increased the opportunities in life for his 5 sons and their mom, Katherine.

During the summer two others took their lives for their own reasons. The last of these deaths in 1999 was my musical companion, Tom Williams' wife, Ise, who died in a car wreck a few days before Christmas of that year. I received a phone call asking for the whereabouts of Tom because his wife had just died and no one knew where he was. I actually had my feet knocked out from under me when I heard this. I knew he was at a gig, so I called there, and I relayed the sad news to him. Ise had been a magical figure in our extended community hosting for many years a week-long women's retreat called Women's Wellness Week on their farm. Her loss was felt by many. Years before, Tom wrote a song for her that appears on *I Always Dreamed of Flying* titled *Timeless Age*. The song celebrates the strength of their time together.

Catch That Ride is my attempt to soften my own death, perhaps with a vision of its context within the many dimensions of being I am aware of. Whether this is a fantasy or not, it will remain up to the attitude I bring to the experience, as it is so with everything in life.

Catch That Ride

When the cool breeze blows on me
I've got the smell of it to set me free and the tide
When there's nothing left but footprints in the sand
And echoes where we held hands oh oh

And high upon the mountaintop
There's a place where heavens starts bye and by
And there's nothing left but clear blue sky
And place where the angels fly oh oh
Where the high wind blows
I'll be happy to catch that ride
With you gazing at the stars by my side oh oh
If teardrops should fall on me
I'll be looking for eternity in your eyes
And there's nothing left for me to do
'Cept keep on loving you oh oh

When I lay down under this canopy
The shadows offered shelter me like your arms
And there's nothing left no songs unsung
No hero looking for his heroine
Oh it'll come one day
And I'll be happy to catch that ride
With you blowing stardust by my side oh oh

During this time in my life, I participated in a local choral group known as the Heartsong Singers. We met almost weekly for many years and worked up a varied repertoire of songs we felt appropriate to share with those who were ill or dying. The group would get permission from family members to enter a home and sing for an individual who was in their last days, usually in hospice care. We also went into the local nursing home and frequently sang there. It was an honor to be a part of this group. I got to revisit my choir days as a baritone/bass.

I have often been accompanied by the knowing of impermanence. My mother often said to me *"this too shall pass."* Buddhist teachings are imbued with references to this characteristic of the nature of reality. While this seems true to me, there is an energy most often referred to as love that escapes impermanence with its universal presence. The song *Loving Seas* concludes the album *Dance When Your Soul Brings You Near*. Part of its message is the line *"of all the parts that make us whole, nothing ever leaves that love has known."* There is a web that makes us whole. Impermanence is a part and love is another.

Loving Seas

There's so many ways to bring the gifts of love inside to shine upon this world
So many ways to see the colors of eternity in view
The passion that we have become to see this world and everyone renewed
There is a way to trust this time and wake our hearts into divine pursuit
  Loving seas will carry this ship back home again
  Loving peace will marry our hearts to the one

Of all the parts that make us whole nothing ever leaves that love has known
There's many textures to explore and gratitude for every shore that's shown
And though the path is rarely straight it gives us time to contemplate and sow
The seeds of understanding, the seeds of what our hearts want us to grow
  Loving seas will carry this ship back home again
  Loving peace will marry our hearts to the one

Making Peace

My father and I had a contentious relationship in my teen years that peaked with a fistfight when I was 15. I honestly don't remember what it was about, but I remember the event. It created a wedge between us that only healed after his death with the realization and acceptance of how much love he had for me, and I for him. My sisters witnessed this fight, and both said it scared them. I didn't beat up my dad. I ended up under a table to escape his wrath. That fight was the last time I partook in a fight with anyone in this life.

The distance between us evolved and in ways got worse when I left home for college. My attempts at communication were met with mixed signals. There was a constant barrage of criticism for my choices and then an occasional expression of concern for how I was doing. Unfortunately for us, there was no seeing eye to eye.

My dad retired from teaching in 1974 at the age of 60. The last three years of his life were characterized by a steady diminishment of his health, likely due to his lung cancer from cigarette smoking. This was a huge issue between him and my mom as he continued to smoke when it was obvious what it was doing to his health. I also smoked for a couple years, but watching his descent into ill health sealed the door on ever picking it up again as a steady habit. At the time of his death, he weighed a scant 90 lbs., and he was hospitalized for most of the last month of his life. Jayn and I were in Sauquoit when he passed but were not able to be with him. I last saw him five days before he died. He passed me a note that said "ayre." How vital is our breath.

He died on the Thursday before Easter Sunday and his memorial service was on the day before Easter. As my father's body lay in the casket, his hands stood out to me—they seemed to still be expressing his strengths. I remember being impressed with the number of folks who showed up to share their condolences. One friend of his in particular, Ralph Briggs, brought me to tears when he stated how much he loved my dad. Many years later, I wrote a song for my dad. It was never recorded but here are the words.

Your Hands

So many days have gone
Since the days I saw you smiling there, showing you cared
And the days turned into years
All the hurts have disappeared, I miss you so sometimes
You would have loved your grandchildren and I know they'd love you
Your great big hands would hold them close with all that they could do

We could have known peace
That I've come to without you, I'm doing my best

The hard words that were said, the way we were both caught in sadness
The years have brought me changes that youth could not inspire
The rebel flag is lowered now
And love is climbing higher yes love is climbing higher

I know you understand what it means to love the land
Making sacrifices to get by
All the things that you could do to teach the young just what is true
Hoping they find a way to make life better
So you showed me about song
How to stand up and be strong in what I know
I still love to play the games
Shoot my jump shot and bowl 10 frames and let the world go
And your wife loves you forever
She still sees you by her side
I am blessed to know her laughter still
In her heart you still reside
In our hearts you still reside

A few years after he died, I had a dream about my father that opened a new door of perception for me about him. In the dream he was dancing while wearing a large sombrero with little yellow balls hanging off the top of the hat. He also had on a large collared white shirt open down to his waist. He turned to me and said, *"I have been Leon, but I've been the lion too!"* It just makes me smile when I recall this dream.

I did not get to participate in my father's death in a manner that felt complete. Years later I became a hospice volunteer. I had a Native American teacher in the 1990's named White Eagle. During one of my many visits to his residence in Winston Salem, North Carolina, he greeted me at the door with the body of a dead owl. He said this was medicine I needed to become familiar with. We did some ritual with the owl energy that led me to seek out a nurse friend who worked for hospice in our area. I questioned her about the volunteer work, and she told me that a training session was beginning in two days that I could sign up for. I took the 11-week training and soon began 7 years of Hospice volunteer work. The relationships that I entered into somehow allowed me to feel the illness and dying process of my father in a way I never could have anticipated.

My first client was a man who was a military veteran. I spent six months visiting this man and his wife once a week. He did not want to die in the veteran's hospital and he actually passed on the steps as they were wheeling him in. He died the same day as my dad passed years earlier, on April 7.

The next individual I worked with was the same age my father would have been if he were still alive. He also suffered from lung cancer, the same as my father. This man's grandson has milled wood for me several times. We had a conversation recently during which I figured out it was his grandfather I had taken care of during his end-days.

The next man I tended in hospice was in the military like my dad. He confessed to me about two weeks before he died that he never wanted to kill anyone, so he always aimed high when he fired his rifle. He had told no one before that moment.

There were several others I worked with during my years as a hospice volunteer. They included a man who had AIDS and another man who was gay in a time when it was not accepted at all. When he died, I inherited his parakeets and took care of them for another 3 years. It was unique to live with birds in my house as well as being surrounded by their songs emanating from the woods outside!

The last official hospice experience I had was with a man named Glenn. Our relationship lasted over three years. We became close friends and I learned much about his family while visiting him weekly. We sat together watching the debacle of 9/11 unfold in 2001. I wrote a song for him and his wife that almost made it onto the album *Stay Above the Radar*, but ultimately didn't make the cut. It was written on guitar and is likely the last song I have composed on guitar.

She Picked Him Flowers

They met in the summer of 34
When life hadn't always been just
But being together soon gave them hope
In the feeling of someone to trust
She'd pick him flowers and dandelion greens
He'd walk to work all alone
Soon they were married and took to a farm

Where they struggled but called it their home

Their firstborn was Vicki and then there was Sue
Children to share in their love
Later when Alice came, she almost died
He felt her pain like a glove
They'd been together for almost 8 years
He was called off to the Great War
For four years their letters were covered with tears
And they prayed a whole lot more

Refrain:
> *They were always together except for the war*
> *They shared everyday hopes and dreams*
> *She picked him flowers he built grandfather clocks*
> *Loved all of their children and right from the start*
> *Hand in hand they filled up their hearts*

He came home determined to do his best
He knew he'd been lucky at sea
He cooked for the soldiers now he built them new homes
Worked with wood so his mind could be free
They reformed their union and swore in those days
They'd always be side by side
The children grew quickly, had lives of their own
My how the days did fly
Refrain:

When you saw them together, you noticed their smiles
The way they could laugh filled a room
But then as it happens, she took to their bed
He was there by her side very soon
But this wasn't easy her body was strong and held on way past her end
When he finally broke down and was first to go
In two weeks she joined him again
Refrain:

I have also worked with two other people who were in the process of dying in more recent years. One was a musician who played the saxophone. He left me a grocery bag full of cassettes that expanded my library of music considerably. A great fun song I found in this treasure chest was *I'm My Own Grampa*, a dizzying lyrical composition. It was performed by Guy Lombardo and the Royal Canadians, a far drift from the rock'n'roll era I was more familiar with. This material fit right in with my slow constant rediscovery of songs and songwriters from the 1920, '30s and '40s. There are many songs from that era that I have come to enjoy performing. I have realized I have a crooner's voice and that material fits me well. There are so many great songs from that era that get re-recorded by current artists, but the songwriters rarely get the credit they deserve. I make an effort to name the songwriter of every song I play that is a cover. It seems like a small justice I can provide!

A RIPENING HARVEST

My next recording, *Red Ripe Apples*, was released in 2009 and I employed many of the same musicians and the same studio with Skip Brown as with the previous album. One addition was a man who joined Grace Note after Martin Scudder and I had our falling out. Jack Bagby played bass and added harmony to the group for eight years and gave us the option of still being a trio. He played bass on this album and was certainly a welcome addition. After Martin and I resolved our acrimony, he also returned to play some fine violin on several cuts on *Red Ripe Apples*.

Grace Note as me, Jack Bagby, and Tom Williams circa 2007.

In many ways this group of songs matured with me as I grew in my musical capabilities. On the cover I wrote *"Sometimes it takes a while for the fruit to ripen. This group of songs reflects some aspects of life coming to a certain maturity through laughter, love, inspiration and finally letting go. That's when the fruit is ready. Enjoy!"*

My musical friend, Sally Walker, inspired the first song, *Cup of Coffee*. She ran a coffee shop in Floyd at the time where I often performed with Grace Note. She shared with me that she wanted to release a CD of coffee songs. I told her I would write one for her, and lo and behold, it happened. Her CD never materialized, but this song did!

The song started while I was driving home from my caregiving job, so I was hastily scribbling lyrics while driving best I could as well. Multitasking isn't the best thing to do while driving but, in this case, I am glad I wrote down the first verse and sang enough of what I was hearing to make the melody become real. I finished it over the next couple of days. *Cup of Coffee* is pretty much a fantasy, as I don't even drink coffee, but many folks have shared how much they enjoyed the song and its lighthearted approach to the topic. The song has a 1920's feel to it, with a mandolin lead that fell into place when I met bluegrass player, Abe Goorskey, while waiting in line to get a pizza. You never know how or when someone new will show up in your life, but pizza and coffee surely attract and reinforce friendship and sharing each in their own way!

Cup of Coffee

Give me a cup, a cup of coffee won't you start my engine please
Give me a cup, a cup of coffee and I'll sail across the seven seas
There ain't nothing like that fine aroma
To get me out of this funky coma
Give me a cup, a cup of coffee ain't nothing gonna bother me

> *When it comes to preparation, few folks will agree*
> *Black or white or cappuccino, espresso or caffeine free*
> *Some folks like their whisky, others sip on tea*
> *But I just gotta tell ya, they don't do much for me*

Give me a cup, a cup of coffee and I'll go the extra mile
Give me a cup, a cup of coffee you know it sure makes life worthwhile
Well there ain't nothing like the guilty pleasure
Of taking some time to enjoy this treasure
Give me a cup, a cup of coffee and you bring me a smile

> *When it comes to conversation, coffee is the best*
> *It warms the passing stranger and welcomes every guest*

> And if you're wanting stimulation, I mean the legal kind
> A little cup of coffee, will do it every time

Give me a cup, a cup of coffee and I'll sing another song for you
Give me a cup, a cup of coffee oh go ahead and bring me two
You can pick me out a 4 leaf clover
But in the morning when you roll me over
Bring me a cup, a cup of coffee
I just gotta have it, I just gotta have it, I just gotta have that brew

Medicine Wheel is the next song on *Red Ripe Apples*. I want to invite you, the reader, to read the lyrics and sense those moments in your life when you have endured difficulties and turned them into something positive. Appreciating the challenges or even injustices in life may or may not be appropriate depending on the circumstances, but they can be learning experiences that guide us on our way.

One friend from my youth inspired me by his presence in the face of the debilitating disease multiple sclerosis. Barney and I grew up two houses apart. He was 2 years older than me and, in many ways, seemed larger than life to me. He had a great voice and soloed several times in our choirs. He was an exceptional athlete though a bit untamed! He also became an excellent drummer. In his late 20's he lived in the Miami area and performed in many bands as well as played percussion in the Miami Symphony. All this changed dramatically in six weeks in his early 30's when he became wheelchair bound by MS for the rest of his life. He managed to live independently until his late 40's when he had to move into a large nursing facility in Utica. Through these years I would visit him whenever I was home visiting my mom. He never complained and was always upbeat even as the disease ravaged onward throughout his body. While at the nursing home he became their official greeter, showing prospective people and their families what was offered by living at this facility. He also wrote two books about his experience with MS. His only relief from the pain was smoking marijuana. This was before CBD and the current understanding of some of the benefits of this herb. He and another man, who had broken his neck diving into one of many old upstate NY quarries, would roll in their wheelchairs out to the back of the nursing home each day to get their relief. The nurses looked the other way, as it was already acknowledged how this benefited many people. Barney passed away in his late 50's after years of dealing with this affliction. His life example was medicine for me and I remain grateful for the moments we shared.

Medicine Wheel

Have you ever looked through the shadows?
Have you ever smiled in the rain?
Have you ever danced on a tightrope or held hands through the pain?
Have you ever stretched past your limit?
Have you ever searched in the dark?
Have you ever crawled on your belly to find your way out?
    Life's a medicine wheel, turning round and round for us to feel
    Every chance you get, make the best of it

Have you ever swung on a gate?
Have you ever soared through the sky?
Have you ever asked the Big Question or told a white lie?
Have you ever howled at the moon?
Have you ever painted the stars?
Have you ever wrote down a poem to find where you are?
    Life's a medicine wheel, turning round and round for us to feel
    Every chance you get, make the best of it
Have you ever dug in the dirt?
Have you ever lingered a while?
Have you ever softened your stance to bring on a smile?
Have you ever perched on a cliff?
Have you ever banged on a drum?
Have you ever wanted a miracle or prayed with someone?
    Life's a medicine wheel, turning round and round for us to feel
    Every chance you get, make the best of it
Life's a medicine wheel. Life's a medicine wheel.

Are You Dreaming Now is a song that I challenged myself to write in a particular manner. I wanted to create a strong, simple piano pattern to carry the song that would blend with the prominent use of a cello. The song is the longest I ever recorded, at 7:18, and for this song the length worked. It has three verses, and it would have been even longer if I had included a fourth verse I wrote. Folks have often asked me what the favorite song I wrote is and, though I don't have a favorite, this would be in the top five.

Are You Dreaming Now

It's a little bit slippery this slope you're walking on
It's a little bit like the mystery of the dark before the dawn
There's something in the fog and smoke that cries to be revealed
There is no definition, no blade that's made of steel
To cut through, to clear away, to resurrect or sway
To make you bleed or make you talk or give yourself away
    Are you dreaming now, of holding someone close
    Of being cast away, of seeing your own ghost
    Are you dreaming now of babies at your breast
    Of journeys to the edge, of slaying your own quest

They're a little bit silly, all these tricks to catch the light
It's a little bit like thunder when the lightening breaks the night
There's something in the rain that falls that frees you from your pain
There is no retribution, no cloth to clean the stain
To soften or hide away, to caution or display
To make you feel or fly about, to give yourself away
    Are you dreaming now of running like a child
    Of choosing what to play, of rapture in the wild
    Are you dreaming now of wearing scarlet robes
    Of feeling just one touch, rejoicing that it's so

It's a little bit like passion when it moves without a course
It's a little bit like the wind on your face when you're straddling a horse
There's something in the breath you take that stokes a holy fire
There is no hesitation, no bell that you require
To listen or run away, to sacrifice or pray
To make you kneel before you rise to give yourself away
    Are you dreaming now of sailing through the mist
    Of fruit pulled from the vine, to savor your first kiss
    Are you dreaming now of waking up yourself
    Of hearing just one sound and laughing at its source
Are you dreaming now?

Heaven's Sweetest Part is the next song on this album. It has a light jazzy feel and, lyrically, is as close as I have ever come to expressing my sense of what being here is really about. This is one of my favorite songs to perform live. This studio version features Randy Anders' smooth brushes on the drums and Gary Everett's saxophone. Gary played on the previous album as well. Both of them always came prepared, which is a gift in itself.

There are also some sweet backup vocals from Sharon Feury in *Heaven's Sweetest Part*. She and I were working together as a duo at this time, with her playing guitar and both of us singing. Sharon was one of the best female guitarists I have ever witnessed play, but unfortunately her shoulder got messed up and she had to give it up. Her performances were always spot on, and she introduced me to much material I would have never played without her urging. Seeing the blessing of everything that comes our way is often not easy. Sharon demonstrated this with grace. There is so much we learn together on this journey and this song speaks of that shared reality.

Heavens' Sweetest Part

When I look in your eyes, I can see the sunrise
The light shining out on me
There ain't nothing to do cept shine with you, and listen to my heart

And the days passing by, my how they fly
Can't hold onto nothing in time
It's just rolling on here and I'm in heavens' sweetest part

> *There's a rose that lives within, that fear and shame can't name*
> *And when it grows, the whole world knows*
> *Its' color from its' flame*

> *There's a rose that lives within, that fear and fame can't tame*
> *And when it shows, the whole world knows*
> *Its' color by its' flame*

As we move on there's laughter and song
And life birthing life constantly
It's amazing what grace fills this place
It's heaven, it's heaven it's heavens' sweetest part.

The title track of *Red Ripe Apples* was written with Sherry in mind. It is a light-hearted romp in the style of a 1920's tune, with piano and saxophone leading the way.

Red Ripe Apples

You could give me red ripe apples
You could give me corn on the cob
But I don't think there's anything sweeter
Than loving right from your arms
You could give me tea from China or fragrances from Kat Man Du
But I don't think there's anything finer
Than cozying up to you
> *Take me to dinner take me to Spain*
> *Take me for a walk in the park*
> *Take me out dancing watch a rainbow in the rain*
> *Cause there's nothing better than the time we share together*

You could give me lottery tickets
A million dollar prize would do
But I don't think there's any bigger winner
Than me when I wake up with you
> *Take me kite flying, scuba diving will do*
> *Take me for ride in your car*
> *Take to England or maybe to France*
> *Cause there's nothing better than the time we share together*

You could take me to the Bahamas
The pyramids or maybe the zoo
But I don't think there's any place I'd rather be
Than right here now with you
You could give me red ripe apples
You could give me corn on the cob
But I don't think there's anything sweeter
Than loving right from your arms

Sometimes there are gremlins in the studio. While recording the next song *Running from the Blues*, Skip Brown and I got one such visit. Skip had recently acquired one of the first 64-track digital recorders to replace his analog unit. It was an experimental board that Skip had a contract with the manufacturer to work out any bugs on. We had just recorded a great track for the organ, and the Hammond player, Michael Randolph, left the studio. Suddenly, *bam!* The entire board shut down and we ended up losing the track. The magic of that track never really reappeared and though what we eventually got was fine, I have always felt something was missing that we couldn't recapture. I am sure that this has happened to a lot of folks. Most studios did not have a logging recorder running all the time to save everything that happened (such as the Beatles had in Apple Studios that yielded added tracks for some of their recordings). All the many tricks of recording via computers and technological advances that have made music so accessible to everyone still don't guarantee the moments that really shine will be always available. We do the best we can!

Running From the Blues

Every time I run away and hide
I start digging round what's left inside
Feels like I'm climbing up a long steep hill
But when I reach the summit, I get the chills
I can see so far away, I can see mountaintops
They look so much like heaven's drops of rain then I look again

Everywhere I go there's push and pull
Spinning round in circles I get through
Some kind of pressure, pressure dropping on down
Squeezing out vestiges of sound
Gonna listen to whales sing, gonna listen to what's missing
Gonna listen to what heaven's silence shows and let go

I keep running, running from the blues
Nothing left but ragged worn out shoes
Gonna stick my bare feet in the sand
Let my heartbeat feel, feel the land
Gonna walk in paradise, gonna change my view
Gonna take another breathe or two and walk with you

In 2008, we all got smacked by some economic realities that proved to pass in time. I wrote *While Rome Falls* during those times. It reflects some of my concerns about where this Western culture is heading. No one really knows, and as I write now there are so many changes afoot that for all of us that perhaps, as this song suggests, *"After centuries of lessons you'd think we would learn a few, like forgiveness, maybe kindness or I am the same as you."*

While Rome Falls

While Rome falls, I think I'll go on humming
While Rome falls, there ain't no use in bumming
While Rome falls, I'll look out for my neighbor
While Rome falls, I'll hope to see you later
When we're picking up the pieces and starting all over again

While our leaders pick our pockets have you checked into their logic
Using fear and fabrication to start conflict between nations
And the people on this planet seem to dream away the days
If they're happy they don't want concerns to get in their way
There's a certain simple madness when the center of one's life
Is the dollar, how to make it, how to take it, how to fake it
And there is nothing that is shinier than winning at all cost
Til you figure in the factor that someone else has lost

While Rome falls, what could be the matter
While Rome falls, go listen to the chatter
While Rome falls, I think I'll move to Paris
While Rome falls, hug someone you cherish
When we're picking up the pieces and starting all over again

And the fires keep on burning turning forests into dust
There are places where the oceans red could make one's heart lose trust
We drill for this and cram for that, insure ourselves from loss
And drive around in hummers to show we're finally boss
There's a beauty and a beast in us and we confuse the two
Using labels like religious, superstitious, well to do
But when it comes to finding what it is that makes us tick
Could it be that feeling good is chasing Moby Dick

While Rome falls, I'll be on vacation
While Rome falls, evolution or creation
While Rome falls, I think I'll write a letter
While Rome falls, I hope it will get better
When we're picking up the pieces and starting all over again

Well the internet is supposed to make us one big family
We sit in little cubbies paying for our liberty
And some hang onto vengeance though it never is enough

To satisfy our hunger we go buy more useless stuff
After centuries of lessons, you'd think we'd learn a few
Like forgiveness, maybe kindness or I'm the same as you
When all the leaves are falling do we rush around with glue
Or just embrace the coming cold and know we can get thru

While Rome falls, Manhattan for a trinket
While Rome falls, could earthquakes really sink it
While Rome falls, nothing is for certain
While Rome falls, go help someone who's hurting
While Rome falls, I think I'll go on Oprah
While Rome falls, got something here to show ya
While Rome falls, I thought I had a dollar
While Rome falls, oops it just got smaller
While Rome falls, I think I'll go on humming
While Rome falls, there ain't no use in bumming
While Rome falls, I'll look out for my neighbor
While Rome falls, I hope to see you later
When we're picking up the pieces and starting all over again

On April 16th, 2007, in nearby Blacksburg at VA Tech, a horrible shooting occurred that took the lives of 33 people. At that same time, the weather was also terrible and two huge pines came crashing down within yards of my house. The sadness that enveloped our communities was palpable for days after. This song was written in response to those events.

Turn Around

We can turn around the damage, turn it into love
Take a chance to see another day
Take a chance to see beyond the tears and the pain
Let love begin again

When the fury of a storm picks up the waves
Or the darkness closes in upon the day
Light another candle, sit close by the fire and pray

We can turn around the damage, turn it into love
Take a chance to see another day
Take a chance to see beyond the tears and pain

Let love begin again

In the beauty of the rose we compensate
Hold onto each other thru our fate
Light another candle, sit close to the fire and pray
We can turn around the damage etc.
In the sky it is written, the sun returns each day
No matter what we do or say

Angel Eyes is the closing song on *Red Ripe Apples*. This song speaks to our collective experience beyond the three-dimensional reality we are so rooted in. It is a song I take to heart, as a reminder to myself of how to be in this moment. It is also a song I should have transposed up a full step. My voice just couldn't reach the lowest notes with any volume. I was stubborn and stuck with the key it was written in. It wasn't until after our final mix and mastering that I really started to question my decision. It turned out fine but I've always felt I could have been more expressive in a different key. When I sing it now, I move it up. Live and learn! As this song says "Life gives you what you ask, you can fly or you can crash! With each wave upon the shore you change some more."

Angel Eyes

May the treasure of your voice and the wisdom of your heart
Rise up in you today with the sweetness of a lark
And the memory of the one guide your senses as you reach
For that place that brings you peace in the feeling of complete

When you hear the red tail sing does it bring tears to your eyes
All these gifts are promising everyone can realize
It's the memory of the one, thru the grace of the divine
Turn your steps into the light with your willingness to shine
Life gives you what you ask
You can fly or you can crash
With each wave upon the shore, you change some more

And the days turn into nights and the nights return the sun
As we dance upon the earth with our laughter we can come
To the memory of the one, letting go we shed disguise
In the presence of each breath, we find our angel eyes

There are four other songs on *Red Ripe Apples*. One is the instrumental, *Breezin' in Blue*. I wrote the song right at the time a close friend lost her daughter in a car wreck. I was asked to play at the memorial service and felt it right to offer this instrumental song. It has a soft lingering quality that is created in part by the cello, played by Erica Lipps on the album. She also was the cellist on *Are You Dreaming Now*.

The other three songs were all recorded previously, but I wanted to give them each a different feel. A version of *Warriors of the World* was recorded live, with the original Grace Note trio accompanied by bass, drums, and electric guitar. *Bring Peace to the World* was originally a cappella and I added instruments and percussion to this chant. Tom Williams added his magical nylon stringed guitar to that song and to *Bad Back Blues*. Bad Back Blues also got some really fine harmonica work by Wes Chapman. Each of these songs became significant additions to the final form of this recording.

From 2007 til 2015, I had the privilege of working as a duo with three different guitarists. Sharon Fury, Cliff Dumais and Bob Dillard are all very talented on the guitar. Sharon and Cliff also added lead and harmony vocals to our arrangements. I learned a great deal playing with these folks and my time playing with each added many songs to my repertoire. Life changes ended each of these duos for different reasons, but I remain grateful for the many hours of musical exploration and growth they provided for me.

Interlude

In June of 2011, my daughter Dolphin got married here at Zephyr. I wanted to write a song for the ceremony. Weeks before our gathering I had a dream that she was getting married in a large spacious church. As she walked down the aisle in the dream, a song was being sung a cappella and that song stuck with me as I awakened. I finished the lyrics and was almost in tears at the beauty of the words. I invited my uncle Bill to sing it with me (he has sung in choirs all his life) and we performed it during the ceremony. During the wedding as the song was being sung, the wind whipped up and rain threatened the gathering on the hill. It eventually subsided, but it was a memorable moment.

There is a Rose

There is a rose with power and joy in it
There is a rose that knows no end
There is a rose that lives inside of us
There is a rose love comprehends

There is a rose of beauty striking still
There is a rose plucked from the stars
There is a rose with fragrance so divine
There is a rose meant for the heart
A rose, A rose, A rose, A rose

There is a rose with passion undefined
There is a rose like dawning light
There is a rose dwells in all humankind
There is a rose made of delight
There is a rose

Staying Above the Radar

    The title track to the last album I have recorded of new songs thus far, *Stay Above the Radar*, was another dream song. I woke up hearing the line "*stay above the radar*" singing in my head. My initial reaction was *what the heck is this?* And the line was so catchy as it sung itself, that I went to the keyboard and the song landed soon thereafter. The musicians featured on this album were members of a band I was playing with at the time, called Reptile DysFunkChen. They are among the most talented musicians I have ever worked with.

    Bob Dillard plays lead guitar on many of the songs on this album. Bob and I played together for two years as a duo, 2 Bob's 4U. Bob has the ability to bring the best out of anyone he plays with. He is innovative and spontaneous in a manner that fed into what I was doing during live performances and on this album. He also has a fine studio he shares with other musicians. We shared many hours jamming and working up tunes in musical exploration. Bob currently plays in a trio called Cocobolo which features much of the writing of Stella Trudel. I had the opportunity to play with Stella and Alan Graf (another fine Floyd musician who recently moved away) in a band a few years ago. I grew to appreciate her songwriting while playing together. There is something that grows inside all of us when we share our creative energies. Music certainly demonstrates that, perhaps better than any other medium.

Reptile DysFunkChen posing for flier photos.
Left to right: Bob Dillard, Jeff Dowd, me, Ralph Brown, Brad Miller

The recording for *Stay Above the Radar* was done at Windfall Studios by Dave Fason. At the time, Dave was living just three miles from my home and the convenience of this was a stark contrast to the many miles I had accumulated traveling to studios in the past. Being in Floyd also made it convenient for the musicians I worked with who were from Floyd as well. Dave has a great listening ear and solid production skills that made *Stay Above the Radar* a fun project. He also plays fine guitar and pedal steel.

The first song on the album, *Just an Exodus,* is a song I discovered when looking through a notebook I keep titled "Songs Not Recorded." The lyrics were there, but I did not recall how to play it as I had not written down chords to work with. I sat down with the keys and soon after it presented itself in an arrangement that I am quite sure was not the original, but possibly even better. There are at least another 70 "songs" sitting in that notebook that will likely remain there—who knows? Bob Dillard and I often played this song during our gigs.

Just An Exodus

Billy said it wouldn't last long this time I swear
Like a really firm handshake or a trip to nowhere
Guess I really didn't know her, didn't know if she'd be there

Billy said life's a mystery and you can take your seat
When the lights go down that's when you feel the heat
I really didn't know her, didn't know if she would dare

She tapped me on the shoulder smiled into my face
She pointed to the mountains said I want to leave this place
Oh I really didn't know her, didn't know if she could care
There are times it's all behind me, yesterday has turned to rust
I don't need no destination, it was just an exodus

Billy called me in the evening said there's been a change of plans
Don't know if I'll get to see you, there's something in the wind
I really didn't know her, didn't know how to prepare

Now I guess it's all behind me turn to someone I can trust
I'd scream out hallelujah, it was just an exodus.

Stay Above the Radar appears twice on the album with its name on the cover. The first recording is a studio version. The second is a live version featuring Reptile DysFunkchen. There is a video online of that version as well. A brief call and return in the refrain of this song is fun to get audiences involved in. This song most likely fits right into the rock 'n' roll category as much as anything I have written. It is always great to see folks dancing to a tune and this song definitely gets people out of their seats!

Stay Above the Radar

My baby's got a fast car, she likes to drive it real far into the night
Sometimes we hit the back roads and places no one else goes
And when she's got the wheel, my seat goes back, and I feel alright
Cause when she's got the wheel, she makes the tires squeal
And it's out of sight
    Cause we stay above the radar, stay above the radar
    My baby drives a fast car we stay above the radar and it's alright

And when we go exploring, we don't' like ignoring what feels right
And sometimes we'll be passing the congestion that happens
Where the lights get too bright
And when we're shifting gears, I feel it right in here and I feel alright
And when we're shifting gears, she whispers in my ear hold on tight
> *And we stay above the radar, stay above the radar*
> *My baby drives a fast car, we stay above the radar alright*

Now if cars could really fly, I know we'd go real high, up to the stars
We wouldn't need no wings cause our propulsion zings
And we can go far
And though we love to roam on our way back home
We wouldn't stop at Venus or Mars
And though we love to roam when we get back home
My baby asks is this a muscle car? And I say yes if we
> *Stay above the radar, stay above the radar*
> *My baby drives a fast car and we stay above the radar*
> *Cause it's alright. Alright!*

I have almost always had at least one cat or dog living with me in my years living in the country. Their companionship is something so many people relish. It is something I have certainly enjoyed as well. I have had sole responsibility for two dogs, Mindy and Prairie, both Border Collie Lab mixes. Other times, my kids or partners have brought their animals into our household, and they are always welcome. Our relationship with these animals has evolved over the centuries. We now must shoulder our responsibility for their well-being—a trade we make for their companionship. The song, *My Friends,* was my attempt to summarize this relationship with our domesticated friends. Dave Fason made the song sweet with his pedal steel and by finding the dog and cat sounds to accent the feel of the song.

My Friends

I got some friends who need a new home
They really need someone who cares
They've hit on tough times, been down on their luck
But which one of us hasn't been there
Some ain't so pretty and one needs a bath

One could be older and blue
    When life is gritty in country or city
    It sure helps to know there's somewhere to go
    And someone who feels you're alright
Now my friends are furry and some of them howl
And some of them might even hiss
There's no need to worry, some have skills that excel
And some of them snuggle and kiss
They make companions walk right into your heart
If you are willing to share
    If you are living in city or town
    It sure helps to know there's somewhere to go
    And someone who misses your sight

And they would say thanks if given the chance
Here's hoping that they will get to
    Cause when life is gritty in country or city
    It sure helps to know there's somewhere to go
    And someone who feels you're alright

Now I might be bragging but I think it's true
My friends could add joy to your life
All their tail wagging and purring for you
Might soothe you in moments of strife
They may be different, but I know they feel
And feelings are what they'll show you
    If you are living in city or town
    When you're on the go it's sure good to know
    There's someone who misses your sight
    If you are living in city or town
    They will be waiting, anticipating
    Someone who's treating them right

Songs have arrived in many different ways over the years. *What Are We Here For* bubbled up out of a simple riff with a bluesy feel. It came to me during my Reptile DysFunkChen years. The band added it to our set list, so I got to share it live with a high energy edge that we pushed along. Ralph Brown and Bob Dillard both added strong leads on the song, live and in the studio.

What Are We Here For

Putting down roots standing in the sun
Stopped looking for trouble cause trouble's no fun
Vibrating like Eden is the coast clear?
Can't see over Jordan cause Jordan's not here
    Rocks and stones might have built thrones
    Or broken bones, what are we here for?
Building up fences keeps us apart
Only does damage to the human heart
Sacrifice mountains and what have we got?
Hard pan and coal dust and choke on the rot
    Feathers and smoke, whiskey and dope
    Some folks need hope, what are we here for?

Some tastes are bitter and liger a while
And then there's chocolate to make us all smile
Famine and fortune, pleasure and pain
Walk with each other, who can explain?
    Sticks and stones might have built homes
    Or mended bones, what are we here for?

Pink lady dancing with the man on the moon
Rock of Gibraltar or salt in the wounds
One day it's flowers, the next day burnt toast
New moon is slumber, full moon we roast
    Incense or lace, we love the chase
    Yours or my place, what are we here for?

At the time *Stay Above the Radar* was being produced, the community of Floyd was fighting the prospects of a gas pipeline running through the heart of the county. A diverse political population occupies Floyd County. (it was the only county to vote for Bernie Sanders in the primaries of 2020 but later Trump carried the county by a 2 to 1 margin) here was significant support for fighting this potential environmental disaster. A basic attraction of the county is that it is situated on a plateau of sorts. All the water here runs out of the county and thus is pretty clean at its source. We also sit on the continental eastern divide with water from our farm running all the way to the Gulf of Mexico while water just a mile to the east of us goes into the Atlantic Ocean. In support of this movement, I wrote this song.

Mountains and Valleys

We build towers of power and hills for the thrills
Climb mountains just for the view
Contemplate, subjugate, prostate and follow
Each of us fills different shoes
So what's it called when one steps on his brother
And what would it feel like to you
Your home place don't matter, your friends all must scatter
Your river gets torn into two, that's what a pipeline would do.

And forests are flattened so someone else fattens
Their wallet on passing gas though
A snake made of metal which won't be so subtle
If it winds its' way near you
And who are the lawyers who prop up destroyers
Of lifetimes of blood sweat and tears
Some folks see dollar signs given to shape their minds
Cash to cover up fears, that's how a pipeline appears
So rally your forces informed by the sources
Of those who have suffered this through
Talk to your neighbors, old timers and strangers
And find out what you can do
Build some compassion for those who have taken on the largest tasks too
Be there to take a stand, reach out your helping hand
Help all to understand, mountains are holy land
No pipeline needs to come through
No pipeline needs to come through, no pipeline, no pipeline

Never Done is a song I wrote for Sandy. There is so much I wish to share about our relationship that I don't know where to start, so I'll start with this song.

Never Done

I tried to be pleasing but that gets too hard
When there's no sense in reason, in fortune or cards
Then the doorway swung open with no effort at all, like a waterfall

What could have been hidden or lost in the tide
Discarded, forgotten or even denied

Was finally welcomed, savored and wide with you by my side

There's no one here left to blame
Evening went, morning came, morning came
No one knows what will come
Love well lived is never done, never done

There won't be another I've stepped out of that ring
You're my friend and my lover, we can share anything
The river's been muddy now it's settled and clear with you here

We don't know what will come
Love well lived is never done, never done, never done

As this song says, *"the river's been muddy now it's settled and clear."* There exists a trust we share about each other's presence that paves the way forward for both of us. For whatever reasons, I've not experienced this radical acceptance on a day-to-day basis before. I am sure that was as much my doing as anyone I was involved with. We both recognize we carry agendas, wounds, feelings of unworthiness and much more that may still bubble up. What has made a huge difference is our ability to recognize those judgments and criticisms and not blame anyone or anything outside ourselves or each other and to talk about these things whenever they arise. One of the favorite phrases we call out to each other almost daily is *"thank you for letting me love you."*

By April of 2010, Sandy was completely moved in with me and our adventure together day-to-day began. Our lives blended fairly quickly. Early in our time together, Sandy ran both the nonprofit, Circle Toward Wholeness, and a landscaping business. I worked with her occasionally landscaping, lending my knowledge of planting and pruning trees. She made use of my skills, brawn, and pickup truck to increase what she could offer. I learned a great deal from her, and we made a great team. I was also still working part time for Wall Residences and had the different aspects of my music, gardening, and demands of a country lifestyle filling up my life.

Sandy has 3 children, who at the time were still living in Indiana, where she had lived for many years. They were in their teens when we met. She was in the habit of visiting them often, driving the eight hours from Virginia to Indiana for years as much as once a month. I occasionally made the trip with her that reintroduced me to Indiana. Eventually I found Chas Cole (from the band in Boston era) living in Brown County, Indiana, and these trips allowed me to rekindle our friendship.

Sandy had formed a friendship with a man who became a second dad for her. Malcolm lived about 2 blocks from where Sandy lived before her divorce. He became a refuge for Sandy while visiting her children, giving her a place to stay without cost and also assisting in the care of her kids and their pet dog, Cayce. He is a most gracious host and has always been most welcoming to me. Malcolm is 94 years old now and still lives independently. We try to visit him every time a trip to Indiana is made. He reminds me of my Aunt Mimi, who is also 94 now and living independently. Both of them are engaged in activities that take them into their communities and both of them have been single all their lives. They are reminders that there are many ways to live meaningful, contented lives.

For many years now, Sandy and I have started our days together with prayer. She shares a Sufi prayer, I share a prayer that has followed me for decades and then we recite the Lord's Prayer in Aramaic, the language that Jesus most likely spoke. Sandy is a Sufi and has studied extensively with Neil Douglas-Klotz who has written many books about Sufism and its relationship to Jesus' teachings. She has attended many retreats and taught workshops covering the Aramaic translation of the Lord's Prayer. It has a substantially different meaning than is presented in most Christian churches of today. I highly recommend Neil Donald-Klotz's many books if you are interested in further exploration.

Camping is an activity that Sandy has enjoyed often in her life. I had not done so much, as I have lived in the woods most of my life. We managed to make camping getaways a part of our summer or fall months for many years. It was during one of those camping adventures that I inadvertently introduced Sandy to her life's calling, Focusing. I have subscribed to a Buddhist magazine titled Tricycle and the day we left for our excursion an issue arrived, so I took it along. Sitting by the campfire, I read an article about a man named Eugene Gendlin and remarked to Sandy that she might enjoy reading this, so I passed it over. When she finished the article, she looked up at me and said, *"This is what I will do for the rest of my life!"* And sure enough she has!

Sandy and I on one of our many hikes

Sandy pursued Focusing by taking classes for the next two years in order to become a certified Focusing Trainer. During that time, we took a trip to California where she attended a workshop in Berkeley. We stayed with a high school friend of mine in Oakland (a great connection renewed with him and another high school friend from the Bay area) and eventually made it down the coast to Big Sur. Combining pleasure and work was good for us both!

Sandy's Focusing work started locally in Floyd, offering in-person classes, and then expanded online. She is now certified as a Coordinator (qualified to train people to teach it as well) and has online clients daily, as well as many classes going all the time. I took her early classes with her, and later from her as well. I now have a regular Focusing partner (Focusing is practiced with a companion) whom I have met with weekly for the last five years. This is very valuable inner work that we share an understanding of. I often assist in her classes and meet with other focusers online in various formats such as workshops or individual sessions.

Watching her commitment to this work has deepened my appreciation for her resolve to be a positive force for change in this world. She is also writing a series of children's/family books called SmartView Stories that share Focusing as a way of being in a community.

Sandy is a lover of music and has many friends who are musicians in Austin, Texas. We traveled there together several times to take in music and visit. Two of her children now live there, so she travels to Texas often (particularly since the addition of her first grandchild).

Another activity we share is dance. We often put on some music and dance, which gets me moving in ways I need to outside of the work mode! Then there is the shared energy and release that music and dance combined provide. This is another moment of gratitude I find myself floating in when I am with Sandy.

She has also upgraded the house I built considerably. From the stone walls behind the house that keep the hill at bay, to the painting of the walls, to many details I likely would ignore, she has encouraged me to make this place a sanctuary. It has been good for me to be pushed a bit in this regard, as I could let things slide too easily. She has contributed mightily to our yard as we now have a large area of berries, fruit trees, and many flower beds surrounding the entire house. I had a good start and others had contributed some, but she took it to another whole level! No longer having a landscaping business, she puts that energy into our yard. There are moments here when I am in awe of the beauty and aromas that exist in our yard. When I pause to take it in, it makes my heart smile!

Another flow of our days together is our relationship to food. It is a pleasure to have good garden food and eggs from our chickens to start our day with. I have always enjoyed cooking breakfast and do so every day. The rest of the day we share meals in whatever way works for both of us. We both share an interest in eating fresh garden foods we can raise and place in storage. A part of every day is spent outside in the gardens most of the year. I also maintain grow-tunnels and hoop beds through the winter that supply us with greens all year round. Since we both work from home now, it is easy to work that out. Having a certain rhythm to the day is beneficial, particularly as we age.

My life is blessed daily with her presence. I will wrap up my thoughts about her with another song I wrote for her early in our time together. It has never been recorded, but here are the lyrics.

I Get to Love You

As you looked into my eyes with each breath we realize
There's a time for seed and flower with the passing of each hour
I get to love you
She whispered in my ear
I get to love you and it's bringing on these tears

In the darkness of the night, what' growing shines so bright
Through the laughter from our souls, this is what we've come to know
I get to love you
In the songs that I will sing
I get to love you and it lights up everything

Like the waves upon the sea, we stretch eternity
With silence in between, we return to touch and feel
I get to love you
As we dance across the floor
I get to love you no words could say more

I can rest now, I am blessed now
Thru the spark of the Divine, it's holier than wine
I get to love you
She whispered in my ear
I get to love you

Our environment is often the cause of people behaving in ways they never would have anticipated. A catastrophe such as a hurricane, tornado or earthquake may cause great suffering and loss of life. Potentially, something is stirred within humans in those circumstances that rivals the best we are capable of. I would love to see that energy rise on a more day-to-day basis. I am not saying our caring for others is missing from our affairs, but the nature of that caring often becomes more inclusive in the face of an environmental crisis. The song *Equalizer* on *Stay Above the Radar* is my attempt to describe those circumstances. There is some fine soprano saxophone provided by Ralph Brown in this song that added to the edginess of the music.

Equalizer

Big storm could be a coming, they say the river could flood
Should be running for shelter, feet are covered in mud
City is filled up with strangers, midnights coming on
Hazards lurk in the shadows, high winds due at dawn

A sad man might drink a potion, madam fingers her pearls
A bad man might rob his neighbor or steal his girl
A rich man thinks he's invisible, poor man got nothing to lose
Preachers selling their Gods while singers wail out the blues

When the wind starts its howling, chaos fills the crossroads
Can't suspend superstition, all the dice have been rolled

Old man sits on the corner, wise man feels some relief
Poets scribble on pages to measure their grief
Young man protects his mother, mad man begs to be free
Romeo and Juliet live in a fantasy

If the water keeps rising, mercy won't know this town
Seems like the eve of destruction, everything is shut down

Thin man slips thru the shadows, lucky man pleas for a break
How many fortunes will this storm take?
Deaf man's hearing a choir, mother clings to her child
Storm's a great equalizer, a chance to reconcile
Reconcile, reconcile

The lone instrumental on *Stay Above the Radar* is *Needle and Thread*. This song came into being during a jam session with Bob Dillard and two of his musical friends, Steve Duiser and T. G. Williams. We met frequently for about a year, sharing many creative moments of song. This jam started as I played a progression and Steve joined in on bass. Bob joined in and T.G. picked up the drums. It bounced around a few times that evening. I worked on it some at home and the next time we got together it really started to take shape. Bob added a short break and some interesting guitar lines that really made the song cook. The third time we got together we recorded a live go at it and the result is what can be heard on the album. The song weaves as a needle and thread would weave in my imagination and builds in energy as it progresses. It is one of my favorite tracks on this album and a monument to the musicianship of Bob, Steve and T.G.

Free With Wings is the next song on *Stay Above the Radar*. It is in memory of my mom. She always greeted me with the words "*Look who's here. It's Bob.*" The phrase was full of enthusiasm, which was how she lived her life. As my partners changed over the years, she never criticized me and always greeted whoever my current flame was with open, loving arms. For this I am very grateful.

After my father died in 1977, my mom continued to live by herself in the house they shared for another 36 years. She was active in community and church affairs and had many close women friends. She loved classical music and traveled to many Elder Hostels around the world. Some of these trips involved listening to opera and classical concerts in Europe. She often traveled with her sister Mary (my Aunt Mimi).

In 2013, my mom had the first in a series of heart attacks that eventually would lead to her death in May of 2014. My sister, Cindy, happened to be visiting home when the first event occurred. Had she not been there, my mom would have likely passed on then. I ended up traveling to Sauquoit shortly after and stayed there with my mom for three weeks while she rehabbed.

My mom, Margaret, and her famous popcorn balls

During that process she conceded she could no longer drive or live unassisted. She had resisted those changes (as many of us do) for several years. My sisters and I were greatly relieved when she agreed to move to assisted living. Mom requested that she be able to live in Elmira, New York, near my sister, Betsey. Within a few days, Betsey found a place for our mother that was in the town where she lived. We were very lucky.

So many interesting and good things occurred in that final year. After the first heart attack my mom was on a ventilator. A nurse in the ICU suggested that some patients liked to listen to music. My sister Betsey replied that she would want to listen to classical music. The first song that came on was *Claire De Lune* by Debussy, a song my mother associated with meeting my father for the first time. She was then moved to the Prentice room in the hospital. Prentice was her mother's maiden last name. Eventually she moved to Maplewood Hall, in the assisted living facility located on Maple Avenue in Elmira. She grew up on Maplewood farm. Circles coming around to greet her and encourage her that this journey would be alright.

Those final three weeks with my mom in the home I grew up in fit in with my caregiving and hospice responsibilities. She was definitely in a weakened and fragile place, but in tribute to the good care she had given herself throughout her life, she rebounded enough to still be able to do much for herself. She was walking several miles many times a week and cross-country skiing as recently as the previous year. She maintained her many connections with her friends as well. Several came to visit her in those last few weeks in Sauquoit. As we were loading the car to leave for her new home in Elmira, one of her closest friends and the mother of a close friend of mine showed up to say goodbye. Seemed like a fitting close to this chapter of her life.

Her resilience persisted through much of her last year but eventually her congestive heart failure became too much to bear. A few months before her death she wondered out loud to me, *"Why am I still here?"* I suspect many people in her situation engage in the same thoughts. Two months before her death, her older brother Steve passed on. I always imagined his passing somehow giving my mom permission to leave as well. At her Memorial service, I played the song *Smile* by Charlie Chaplin, as her smile could light up anywhere. I also read a poem I wrote that goes as follows.

The Little Things
For my Mom

It's the little things that mothers do
Like hold your hand or tie your shoes
It's the little things that never stop
The welcome smile and the place to flop
The walk around the park on showery days
The planting of the seeds in the month of May
It's the little things that mothers do
Like make eggnog or cheer for you
The little things that no one else can see
Unrecognized by you or me
The band-aid on the furrowed wounded brow
The times with little sleep and wondering how
Most little things blend and disappear
Like lullabies or whispers in the ear
It's the little things that make a life
A man, a husband, a woman, a wife
And all the little things combine for us to see
A life well lived is little things from A to Z

Free With Wings has a classical feel. The tone is perhaps sad, as I was likely still grieving this loss. This song is simple in performance with just piano, violin and vocals.

Free With Wings

Many years in between a child was born and then left this dream
And what a dream a memory set upon her soul
Of song and wind and mountain trails
Of fireflies, 7 hills and vales
What a place she chose to be, savored by her soul

Country roads and waterfalls, literature and concert halls
What a heart free with wings welcomed by her soul

   All of our ancestors gone on before
   Sorrow and joys left behind
   Think of the good times that we always had
   Savoring those who were kind

Many years passing thru, a first breath and last one too
All she left for us to care, may we do it well
Simple things since she's gone come to me at the dawn
What a smile for all to see greet eternity

Free with Wings differs greatly from anything else on the album. It is certainly different from the preceding song, *Needle and Thread,* that is soaring in its progressive rock quality. This is another example of how difficult it is for me to answer the question, *"What genre is your music?"* To give people an expectation of what it is they will hear really isn't fair to the listener or the musician. My answer will probably always be *"It depends on which song you're asking about!"*

Perhaps the biggest gift my mom left behind was uniting my two sisters and me in caring for her. The process involved travel for Cindy and me, and a significant amount of more day-to-day interaction for Betsey. Being around my mom and them both more frequently allowed for conversations and revelations to occur that might otherwise have remained dormant. I have seen this happen in my hospice work and it certainly occurred for us. Everything can be cherished here, as the desert and the jungle are both assets in the total balance of life as we know it.

The next song on *Stay Above the Radar*, titled *River of Song,* I wrote for my two daughters, Amy Sunshine and Dolphin Moon. They are both thriving in different ways in this life. Their presence (near or far) has been a gift that I never could have anticipated. Like so many members of my family, they have both entered the academic world that I declined to participate in. I am glad they have found meaningful employment on that path. They have contributed three grandchildren to my experience as well, and that has its own significance. This song rocks out and is one that I have played occasionally solo over the years.

Dolphin and Amy, circa 1982

River of Song

Look out your window, look at the dawn
So much redemption coming on
It's like a river, a river of song
And this one's for you after I'm gone

Live for the moment, live for the truth
Promise to never pass by the youth
With every lesson, there is no wrong
When you are living in a river of song

Refrain:
    A river so deep, a river so wide
    It carries your fortune and memories inside
    A river so swift you can't comprehend
    Where it is going, what lies round the bend

Look at the mountains, sail on the seas
Live the adventure, the sweet mystery
All of these places are calling you on
When you set foot in the river of song

And if you're hungry and won't be denied
You've turned every corner, nothing left inside
That's when you find it, and further along
Share it with someone, this river of song
Refrain:

Look out your window, look at the dawn
So much redemption coming on
It's like a river, a river of song
This one's for you to carry on

This one's for you to carry on
It's like a river, a river of song

The last song on this album is the reprise of *Stay Above the Radar* performed live by Reptile DysFunkChen. It is a more acoustic version that was recorded when the band played for an event at Dogtown in Floyd. It is the only song I ever reprised on an album.

Pressing Rewind

The last album I have released to date is called *Rewind*. I was warned that if I didn't get my early cassettes transferred to digital, the tapes would at some point become nonfunctional. Sometime around 2010, Skip Brown assisted me with that transfer. I held onto the material until I realized I wanted to put what I thought was the best of those early cassettes out there as a CD. Dave Fason engineered the final selections into a CD format. We also embellished a few songs by adding a few tracks. This became possible with the advent of recent computer programs. Here is a listing of the songs from *Rewind*. The songs with vocals I have already shared the lyrics to previously in this musing.

01 The Choice / Rise up Singing
02 The Treasure
03 Welcome the Way
04 Camels Hump - instrumental
05 Live Inside a Body
06 Love Belongs
07 A Child Was Born
08 Daddy Long Legs - instrumental
09 Jumping up and Down Together
10 Light in the Wind
11 I Love You Friend
12 Waterfall - instrumental
13 Laughter and Tears
14 Release Me
15 You've Given Me
16 Circles Returning

During the last few years, I have often gotten together with musicians to jam. Those sessions have mostly occurred at Brad Miller's home, the drummer in Reptile DysFunkchen. He records everything we do and sends it to us a few days later for possible upgrading to songs. Recently, I have written the lyrics to several songs via this method. Between the Reptile DysFunkChen years and these more recent songs, there are likely 15 songs that could be recorded and released. Here are the lyrics to two songs written last year. The first, *Stepchild of Attack*, was written during the U.S.

withdrawal from Afghanistan. The second, *Red Flag Alert*, is a kicking rock tune that is a blast to perform and may see some daylight soon.

Stepchild of Attack

Stand in line, settle down, by morning you'll be gone
The summer sun is setting fast, the evening cooling down
Gazing as the light goes out, another world could rise
Holding onto to documents, pleading with their eyes
Who was nameless on the hill standing in the mist
Who was looking back to east and raising up a fist
Who was shadowed in the dark by demons on the run
Who forgot the words of tears live in everyone
Come over here, come over here there's no going back
Come over here, come over here you stepchild of attack

Outside the world feels burnt by screams of being left alone
The old stonewalls cannot be changed into another home
The spirit of your ancestors will follow on your trail
The nightingales will sing their song when you finally set sail
Who was blameless on a hill standing in the dark
Who was looking to the west for a vital spark
Who was waiting for the sun of another day
Who was praying for a chance to live another way
Come over here, come over here there's no going back
Come over here, come over here you stepchild of attack

Red Flag Alert

It's late at night the moon is full
The cards are down it's been a duel
The price is high, got dirty dreams
The hooting owl is set to scream
    Red flag alert, no one, no one gets hurt
    Red flag alert, no one, no one gets hurt

The prince of joy has called my name
We walk outside, stand by a flame
Can't ere no more, it's an uphill climb
Ain't got no ticket in this paradigm

Red flag alert, no one, no one gets hurt
Red flag alert, no one, no one gets hurt
You can count to three, down on bended knee
Rocking all night long
Have a fiery heart, chasing all you've lost
Like a one-night stand
Red flag alert

Another additional song I recently wrote that we have added to the jam band repertoire is *Human Disgrace*. As a songwriter my task can be to reflect the cultural myth as it appears, without the sugar coating available in so much media these days. I have mentioned Leonard Cohen before and again I wish to thank him for his inspiration providing me with inner permission to explore both the light and the dark of these times.

Human Disgrace

Broken laws and broken treaties
Broken vows and broken thesis
Little men in high places
Golden smiles upon their faces
Oh, they're all over the place
Oh, it's a human disgrace

Busted cops and funky judges
Dusted crops and no one budges
Who is weak and who is strong
Who is bent to get along
Oh, they're all over the place
Oh, it's a human disgrace
   Where are we going, where have we been?

Unanswered questions stretch our limits
Politicians lie and fidget
We dump trash into the oceans
We speed and crash can't stop the motion
Oh, we're all over the place
Oh, it's a human disgrace

CASTING SEEDS TO THE WIND

In the late fall of 2018, I was setting up to perform an evening of songs at a local restaurant and hotel when I heard a voice say, *"Can we help?"* I turned around to discover my sister Cindy, her husband Dan, and my niece Megan, standing there. It was a huge surprise as they came unannounced from Maryland to visit and hear me play (a 5 1/2-hour drive). This was the first time anyone from my family had ever heard me play a three-hour gig and I felt incredibly honored by their presence. It also turned out to be the last gig I played for the next three years as I intentionally decided to take a break from gigging and then Covid hit, which changed so many of our lives.

I stopped playing music almost altogether and let myself discover reading novels again and pursued learning to draw. When I was young, I was informed by my sixth-grade teacher that I had no drawing skills. It was the only class I ever got less than an 'A' in during elementary school and deservedly so. My stick figures barely looked like stick figures. I obtained a copy of the book *Drawing on the Right Side of the Brain* by Betty Edwards and through following her instructions, I slowly discovered I actually could draw! It was a tremendous revelation! This has given me a different perspective on how I view the world through these two eyes. It also created the opportunity for me to draw when I am with my grandchildren.

Sketch of my porch

As I travel further on life's highway, there is a sense of contentment that permeates most of my days and nights. I jump in and out of musical endeavors and connections. The simplicity of just sitting and playing the piano returns almost daily, and I am singing again. There is a local antique store in Floyd called Chic's that has an old beat-up piano that plays like a dream. I often go there on Saturdays and let the good times roll. People aren't expecting music when they arrive at Chic's, so there are many interesting interactions between myself and the clientele.

There have been three wonderful reunions in the past three years with the band from Boston, my college roommates. We gathered at Rick Wilstermans' beautiful home in Chatham, Massachusetts, for the first two. It was an amazing time I referred to as *Eat, Play, Nap!* Chas Cole, Bob Tschilske and I have continued making music most of our lives. Rick bought a drum set for the occasion and sharpened his strokes. We had a blast running through old familiar tunes and new material some of which we had written. We couldn't find the Woodard Brothers, but recently, after the second reunion, they found us. Unfortunately, they were unable to attend this year's festivities. This summer the four of us got together again in Bloomington, Indiana near Chas for another week of music, revelry and plain old good times! Travel isn't as easy as it used to be, but the strength of our heart connection shines when we are together, making it well worth the effort. Over 50 years later it is quite remarkable. I absolutely feel blessed to be alive every minute we share. We actually got a lot better this

The boys, reunited: Bob Tschilske, Chas Cole, Rick Wilsterman, and me

time knocking out some great blues tunes and a bunch of 60s and 70s music we challenged ourselves with. I wrote this song during our first time back together. After 3 years of playing it, it's sounding pretty good! The lyrics attempt to summarize our time together.

Playing Our Songs Again

Many years ago, in a distant land
Some young gentlemen formed a rocking rock and roll band
They took a chance on a different way
Rolled the dice and learned how to play
Burned the nightlights to keep their dream alive
Refrain:
> *We got to play, we got to sing*
> *We got to do the very thing*
> *That brings us here and makes us smile*
> *That makes this living all worthwhile*
> *There's been tears and laughter too*
> *And hard times that we got thru*
> *Now we're here to play our songs again*

And as the years rolled by
So many changes on the fly
The path looks like a long, long river's bend
Don't know what will come next
It'll probably be complex
And we know it'll all work out in the end
Refrain:

I really don't know what tomorrow will bring in the musical frame of my life. Perhaps that is best, as I am open to being surprised. I live in a community that is full of musicians capable of so many different genres of music so there is always possible interaction on tap. So many other activities still call out to me, and I respond as best I can. This is true of most musicians, as we tend to mix careers in music with other jobs, family, friends and creating a balance in the responsibilities of life in the 21st century. These are some words that have resonated with me all my life from the Tao Te Ching by Lao Tzu.

Be content with what you have
Rejoice in the way things are
When you realize there is nothing lacking
The whole world belongs to you

A few days ago, I received an email from a man who found a copy of the *Celebration Space* cassette in a thrift store in Ithaca, NY. He was very interested in learning who was involved in its creation and offered to digitize the copy he had and send it to anyone who replied. What followed was a series of emails shared by many of the folks who contributed to its making. I was blown away by the synchronicity of his finding and offering. I did not possess the music that was on this recording. He sent me a WAV form that I then downloaded and listened to. It was this cassette that set my feet on the recording path I have shared with you throughout this book. For it to show up at this moment added a sense of completion I never would have guessed could be possible.

Here I am in delight and surprise,
    rising up again to guide my way on.

EPILOGUE

Several important people in my life have left this dream since I began this project. Robin Paris, Diana De Simone, Sharon Feury, Jack Bagby, and very recently Leaf Salem have re-entered the Spirit realm. My heart has been grieving in ways I cannot really explain. Perhaps I have slowed down a bit as I find myself pausing frequently to say thank you to them and others who have passed on. AND, also to just listen and feel the immense energy that pulses through this human experience I am part of.

There have been moments when I could not say thank you often enough. The gifts of sincere friendship, enduring love, musical enthusiasm, shared bounty, safe surroundings, good health, and creative promise persist in my life.

Along with the writing of this book, I have recorded a new full band version of the song I Always Dreamed of Flying. Three very talented musicians joined me for this mini project, Dave Owen on bass, Fred Harris on drums and Kayce Caveman Jones on guitar. We worked together in Dave Fasons Windfall studio! It is available for listening on the usual streaming services.

Recently I heard a new song by Bill Champlin (a favorite song writer of mine). There is a line in the song that jumped out to me. *"Music is the perfect path to love."* I sense the daily reality of this merger of love, music, and life. I am blessed to participate in this sacred circle. In this beautiful world, here I am.

"Living all in kindness, sharing one destiny.

Living all from the generosity of Love's unbroken circle."

~from *Fragrance of the Rose*

You can find me at Chic's on the weekends, still playing

Bonus Material

The Recordings

Treasures in the Stream, 1987, cassette only

Side A:
- 01 The Treasure
- 02 Strong Foundation
- 03 Star Eyes
- 04 The Choice
- 05 Live Inside a Body

Side B:
- 06 One Part (You Don't Gotta Be Wild)
- 07 Daddy Long Legs
- 08 Freedom Eyes
- 09 A Child Was Born
- 10 I Love You Friend

Circles Returning, 1989, cassette only

- 01 Circles Returning
- 02 Jumping Up and Down Together
- 03 Waterfall
- 04 Release Me
- 05 Laughter and Tears
- 06 Welcome the Way
- 07 Dance in the River
- 08 Camel's Hump
- 09 The Fool
- 10 Love Belongs

Light in the Wind, 1990, cassette only

Side A:
- 01 Step Lightly
- 02 Light in the Wind
- 03 This is the Place
- 04 Four Winds
- 05 Wheels Turn
- 06 My Only Purpose
- 07 Welcome the Way
- 08 I Will Not Try
- 09 Give Up My Defenses

Side B:
- 10 Walk, Walk, Walk
- 11 Bring Peace to the World
- 12 Gifts
- 13 We Can Shine
- 14 Laughter and Tears
- 15 Dance in the Light
- 16 I am Sustained (by the Love of God)
- 17 You've Given Me
- 18 You Know Hu

Lifetimes and Ages, 1991, CD and online

  01 Awakening/This Journey
  02 Lifetimes and Ages
  03 Redeemer's Gate (Instrumental)
  04 Hallelujah Song
  05 Keep My Heart Open
  06 Warriors of the World
  07 Calling Calling
  08 Go Lightly

I Always Dreamed of Flying, with Grace Note, 1993, CD and online

  01 I Always Dreamed of Flying
  02 Strong Foundation
  03 Freedom Rise
  04 The One, The Dream, The Dance
  05 Nightshades
  06 Crossroads
  07 Riding the Dragon
  08 Dragonfly
  09 Timeless Age
  10 Live Inside a Body
  11 Freedom Eyes
  12 For Everyone

Keep the Light Burning, 1997, CD and online

  01 Who Knows What Will Come
  02 Steppin' Into Heaven
  03 Pulse of Life
  04 I Want to Thank You
  05 Harmlessly Beautiful
  06 Tears Will Roll Away
  07 The Message
  08 The Key
  09 Picture This
  10 Pray for Each Other
  11 Keep the Light Burning

Fragrance of the Rose, with Grace Note, 2001, CD and online

  01 Sail
  02 Always There is Love to Give Away
  03 Squirrel Hill
  4 Fragrance of the Rose
  05 Openly Be
  06 Bad Back Blues
  07 What's Dear
  08 Everyone of Us has Got a Name
  09 Great Big Love
  10 Something to Believe In

11 *So You Dance*
12 *Gift to Be Simple*
13 *Love Grow Slow*
14 *Somewhere Over the Rainbow*
15 *Love Will Leave You Whole*

Rivers from the Sun, 2005, CD and online

01 *Eagle Flies at Dawn*
02 *Sunrise on the Shore*
03 *Divinity's Way*
04 *Ode on a Hill*
05 *Waltz of the Lily*
06 *Siren's Song*
07 *Butterfly*
08 *Nightshades*
09 *Mediterranean Dream*
10 *Voices in the Wind*
11 *Clear Blue*
12 *Rivers from the Sun*
13 *Homeward Bound*

Dance When Your Soul Brings You Near, 2006, CD and online

01 *Dusty Pillow*
02 *Something About It*
03 *Love Is Like A Mirror*
04 *Aching Blue*
05 *Making Shadows Out of Me*
06 *I Am Amazed*
07 *Dance When Your Soul Brings You Near*
08 *This Beautiful World*
09 *I'm in You and You're in Me*
10 *Your Love*
11 *Good Time Blues*
12 *Catch That Ride*
13 *Without Tomorrow*
14 *Loving Seas*

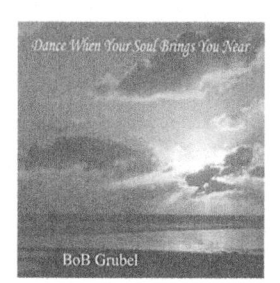

Red Ripe Apples, 2009, CD and online

01 *Cup of Coffee*
02 *Medicine Wheel*
03 *Bad Back Blues*
04 *Are You Dreaming Now*
05 *Heaven's Sweetest Part*
06 *Red Ripe Apples*
07 *Warriors of the World*
08 *Breezin' in Blue*
09 *Running from the Blues*
10 *While Rome Falls*

11 Turn Around
12 Bring Peace to the World
13 Angel Eyes

Stay Above the Radar, 2015, CD and online

01 Just an Exodus (feat. Bob Dillard)
02 Stay Above the Radar (feat. Ralph Brown)
03 Riding the Design (feat. Bob Dillard)
04 My Friends (feat. Dave Fason)
05 What Are We Here For (feat. Ralph Brown & Bob Dillard)
06 Mountains and Valleys
07 Never Done
08 Equalizer (feat. Ralph Brown)
09 Needle and Thread (feat. Bob Dillard)
10 Free With Wings
11 River of Song
12 Stay Above the Radar (Live) [feat. Ralph Brown]

Rewind, 2016, CD and online (selected material from *Treasures in the Stream, Circles Returning* and *Light in the Wind*)

01 The Choice / Rise up Singing
02 The Treasure
03 Welcome the Way
04 Camels Hump
05 Live Inside a Body
06 Love Belongs
07 A Child Was Born
08 Daddy Long Legs
09 Jumping up and Down Together
10 Light in the Wind
11 I Love You Friend
12 Waterfall
13 Laughter and Tears
14 Release Me
15 You've Given Me
16 Circles Returning

Creative Friends

Here are the websites for or links to some of the wonderfully creative people who have blessed my path in this life.

Alan Graf
    https://alienbeing.hearnow.com

Bill Deats - amazing artist
    https://www.linkedin.com/in/bill-deats-06661b61

Cliff Dumais
    https://cliffordjames.org

Danny Britt
    https://reddawgmusic.com/

Dave Fason – Windfall Studio
    https://soundcloud.com/dave-at-windfall-studios

Isa Graefe - artist
    https://www.facebook.com/isamariamagic

Jayn Avery – potter
    https://www.etsy.com/shop/blueheronpottery

Jill Schneider – healer
    https://jillaynschneider.com

Jim Scott
    https://jimscottmusic.com

John Sledd
    https://sledd.com

Katherine Chantal
    https://www.facebook.com/LifeCeremoniesByKatherine

Lee Stone - artist and healer
    https://www.leestone-art.com

Martin Scudder
    https://www.allmusic.com/artist/martin-scudder-mn0002549156

Peter Handler - Handler Studio
    https://www.handlerstudio.com

Richard Allen - features custom-made chandeliers, wall sconces, tables & more
    www.richardallenlights.com

Sandy Jahmi Burg
    www.learnfocusing.org

Skip Brown - Final Tracks Studios
    https://www.manta.com/c/mxfz1rt/final-track-studios

Starroot - artist
    http://starroot.com/wb/pages/home.php

Stella Trudel
    https://stellatrudel.com

Tom Williams – The Santa Cares Project
    https://www.facebook.com/SantaCares

Victoria Stone
    https://www.amazon.com/stores/Victoria-Jordan-Stone/author/B001JPBSE2

Kayce Caveman Jones
    BenevolentWind@gmail.com

Vital Characters

Family of Origin

Leonard Grubel – dad
Margaret Grubel – mom
Betsey – sister
Cindy – sister
Uncle Bill
Uncle Steve
Aunt Mimi
Guy Johnson – grandfather
Elsie Johnson – grandmother
Lillian Grubel – grandmother

Current Family

Amy – daughter
Dolphin – daughter
Grandchildren
 Fisher
 Watson
 Pearl
Sandy Jahmi Burg – partner

Zephyr Family

Jayn Avery
Tom Franko and Jody Franko and children
Katherine Chantal and children
Ray Chantal (deceased)
Diane Giessler and children
Dick Giessler (deceased)
Perrin and Jenny Heartway and children

Partners Through the Years

Jayn
Katie
Dee
Cate
Sherry
Sandy Jahmi Burg

Musicians

I was blessed to play with these musicians and many more over the years, all of whom contributed to my musical evolution. My biggest gratitude to every one of you for your love of and devotion to music has lit up my path.

Melted Cheese – the Boston band
    Chas Cole – bass
    Martin Woodard – guitar
    Rick Wilsterman – drums
    Bob Tschilske – guitar
    Doug Woodard – drums
    Bill Guffey - keyboards
Tom Williams – Grace Note –acoustic guitar and vocals
Martin Scudder – Grace Note –violin and vocals
Gerry Skendarian – Grace Note - bass
Jack Bagby – Grace Note – bass and vocals
Frank Greenlee – recording engineer –guitar
A'Court Bason - recording engineer –percussion
Jarvis Dreaming - recording engineer –guitar
Skip Brown – recording engineer- guitar
Dave Fason – recording engineer, guitar and pedal steel
Billy Bell – saxophone
Chris Prokosch – bass
Sally Walker – backup vocals
Kari Kovic – backup vocals
Sharon Feury – guitar and backup vocals
Rio Simione – congas and backup vocals
Abigail Bowen – backup vocals
The Celebration Singers
Randy Anders – drums
Erica Lipps – cello
Charlie Howe – cello
Gary Everett – saxophone
Mike Mitchell – violin
Michael Randolph – Hammond organ
Wes Chapman - harmonica
Jay Amman – Hammond organ
Bob Dillard – guitar
Ralph Brown – saxophone
Brad Miller – drums and percussion
David Annerelli – bass
Janiah Allen – drums and percussion
T.G. Williams – drums
Steve Duiser – bass
Cliff Dumais – guitar and vocals
Gary Collins - vocals
Alan Graf - guitar
Fred Harris - drums
Dave Owen - bass
Kayce Caveman Jones - guitar and drums

Made in United States
North Haven, CT
06 November 2023